PRAISE FOR FADUMO KORN AND
BORN IN THE BIG RAINS

"A searing portrait of female genital mutilation in Somalia . . . [translator] Levin suggests that reading groups look into their own lives to ask themselves whether any of their own cherished beliefs have been proven wrong or destructive. If so, what happens in these pages may not seem so alien—but no less appalling."
—*Kirkus Reviews*, Third Annual Book Club-Reading Group Issue

"[W]hat brings truly sustainable change is the courage of individuals like Fadumo Korn to move from survivors to impassioned advocates for justice. This book helps us all to understand how such a transformation is possible."
—Noeleen Heyzer, United Nations under-secretary-general and former executive director of the United Nations Development Fund for Women (UNIFEM)

"[Born in the Big Rains] is a moving story of the suffering, struggle, resilience, and redemption of one remarkable individual whose indomitable spirit, innate virtue, and unfailing love for others transform her into a social activist, committed to ending female genital mutilation and helping those who continue to suffer its consequences."
—Dr. Mirta Roses, director of the Pan American Health Organization (PAHO)

BORN IN THE BIG RAINS

A Memoir of Somalia and Survival

By Fadumo Korn

With Sabine Eichhorst

Translated from the German and with an
Afterword by Tobe Levin

The Feminist Press
at the City University of New York
New York

The Feminist Press at the City University of New York
The Graduate Center
365 Fifth Avenue, Suite 5406
New York, NY 10016

Originally published under the title GEBOREN IM GROSSEN REGEN © 2004 by
Rowohlt Verlag GmbH, Reinbek bei Hamburg

The Library of Congress has catalogued the cloth edition as follows:

Korn, Fadumo, 1964-
  [Geboren im großen Regen. English]
  Born in the big rains : a memoir of Somalia and survival / by Fadumo Korn with Sabine
Eichhorst ; translated from the German by Tobe Levin.
  p. cm. — (Women writing Africa)
  ISBN: 978-1-55861-578-6 (pbk.)
  ISBN: 978-1-55861-531-1 (trade cloth)
  1. Female circumcision—Somalia—Case studies. 2. Female circumcision—Somalia—
Psycological aspects. 3. Somalia—Social life and customs. 4. Korn, Fadumo, 1964- 5.
Somalis—Germany—Biography. 6. Women, Somali—Germany—Biography. I. Eich-
horst, Sabine. II. Title. III. Series: Women writing Africa series.
  GN484.K6613 2006
  392.1096773—dc22
  2006010520

This publication was made possible, in part, by the Rockefeller Foundation.

Text and cover design by Lisa Force
Printed in Canada

13 12 11 10 09 08   5 4 3 2 1

Contents

*To my beloved sister, Khadija,
and to my husband, Walter, and
son, Jama Philip, who have
always given me their full support.*

Nomadic Life

1

In the distance, a lion roared, deep and long, dismissing the night. The air smelled of smoke and freshly brewed tea, and on the horizon the day's first light chalked the sky. My shoulder soaked up the warmth of Adan's breath, still coming in even puffs. Rubbing the sleep from my eyes, I sat up.

Only a few paces away my mother squatted, cracking twigs. Maryan, Uncle Yusuf's second wife, rolled up the mats. A metal suitcase, two stools, a pail, and cooking pots stood where our hut had been the previous evening. The lion roared again, this time briefly. Soon he'd find himself a place to sleep. We had survived the night.

Aunt Maryan began to undo the colorful woven leather bands that usually decorated our huts. My cousin Nadifo bundled branches, and in the distance I heard the wooden sound of a camel's bell. My brother Adan awoke. I took his hand. In a few hours, once the sun stood higher in the sky, the sand would glow like copper. Now, in the half dawn, silhouettes of shrubs resembled spiky hills. The brush had been driven across the desert, rolling about before finally being abandoned, as though Allah had been throwing dice and had tired of the game. Here and there an acacia tree stood out.

My mother fanned the fire to flame. Then she carried the kettle to one of the water containers and filled it. Adan stretched and secured his loincloth, getting up so I could roll up our mat. My mother poured a little water into the hole Adan had dug in the sand so that he could wash his face. She then turned to me. I loved the fresh coolness of water on my morning skin.

A fence made of thorny twigs surrounded the camp and confined our camels. I heard my brother Jama's tongue clicking at the herd. The bells now rang out clearly too, and the air vibrated with penetrating animal calls. I placed our rolled-up mat next to the others.

I didn't want to move away. I wanted to stay with my friend Mahad.

A sheep bleated, and Nadifo poured tea into a cup. My father entered the half circle in front of our huts and called out to Adan, who ran to Timiro, Uncle Yusuf's first wife. In a minute he returned with Timiro's sons. Jama herded a number of transport camels in our direction as he clicked and with his staff coaxed their flanks. Two female camels tried to bite him, but Jama sidestepped the attack. They answered with long throaty complaints—threatening, almost menacing announcements of displeasure.

"Ju," my father said, tugging at their reins to make them kneel while the boys brandished their sticks. "Ju," my cousin Saïd called as well. Though resisting, the first animal bent its knees and let its weight sink to the earth, its long neck stretching its head high. The other camels were also biting, spitting, and complaining, but my father, Saïd, and Jama weren't the least bit bothered. Finally they had the camels seated on the sand in front of the huts. The leathery skin on the animals' legs was dusty brown.

The men began to examine the herd with tender hands: stroking their necks, torsos, and backs, feeling for leeches and ticks, checking legs for thorns and hoofs for stones. They then spread mats over the camels' backs, stroked them flat, and took great care to eliminate even the slightest unnecessary pressure or irritation. Gradually, they loaded the camels with everything we owned. A nomad never owns more than can be loaded onto his camels' backs.

3

A hand gripped my arm. "Go and milk the goats," my mother said. Taking the wooden pail, I wove my way through the camels to the makeshift fence. Careful not to pierce myself on thorns, I opened the gate. I smelled dung, and a high-pitched whining filled the air. The goats nuzzled my legs, some using their horns. I could feel their breath through my clothes. I counted them to make sure none had gone missing during the night and then squatted beneath the udders of one unhappy, squealing goat. Deftly, I clamped one of her legs between my knees and began, tenderly, to stroke her udder and pull on the nipple. But at first no milk came. The animal refused, knowing that we were on the verge of moving.

Returning with the half-full can, I found all the other huts had been dismantled and Jama had tied the forelegs of the loaded camels to prevent their running away. My mother filled a cup and handed it to my father, then passed it to my brother and to me before she drank what was left of the warm milk.

Mahad. Where in the world was Mahad?

The sun hovered over a hill when the caravan set off. Hoofs sank into the sand, and lambs bleated. Camels snorted, gargled, and brayed. My father had bound the jaw of one of the females to prevent her from biting. In a long row, the camels passed along the thorn fence that guarded what had once been our home.

Jama guided the lead animal. Behind him, Saïd and Uncle Yusuf's sons drove the herd, brandishing sticks, clucking, and pulling on the ropes tied to the animals' halters. Every once in a while one of the boys would imitate Jama's clucks. Nadifo and the other girls tried to keep the goats and sheep together.

I sat in the sand next to the spot that had served as our fireplace and watched the caravan leaving.

"What's the matter?" my father asked when he spied me sitting there.

"I'm staying here."

My father leaned over toward me and looked down. "My daughter is staying here?"

"I'm not going! I want to stay with Mahad."

Mahad and I belonged to the same clan and were distantly related. Mahad was my age and not very well liked because he could neither hear nor speak. But that didn't bother me. We had found a language in signs and gestures. I liked Mahad and didn't want to leave him behind. He was my friend!

My father shook his head and rejoined the caravan.

The lead animal struck off, followed by the others laden so high with goods that they dwarfed their drivers. Barefoot women and small children marched along over the steppe, wrapped in cloth for protection from the sun. I stared at the cloud of dust that grew tinier and tinier, still visible long after all the human and animal noises had faded. I pulled my wraparound tighter. A fly crawled up the inner side of my forearm.

The sun rose higher. I was sweating.

Over the horizon, the dust had vanished.

Soon, I began to feel frightened.

I started to cry. From anxiety and rage, I ripped off my scarf and threw it on the glowing embers. In seconds it blazed. I was too proud to run after the caravan, but no one had come back to get me. My family had moved on and simply left me behind!

I looked around. In the shadow of an acacia, only a few paces away, were Mahad's family's huts. Everything was silent. At this hour Mahad's sisters and cousins were watching the goats, while he and his brothers were leading the camels to water. They wouldn't be back before nightfall.

I sat in the hot sand crying, waiting.

Hours must have passed before I spied another sand cloud, smaller this time, moving in my direction. Once it had gotten close enough, I recognized my father.

"How can a child be so stubborn?" he complained. "You can't stay. We've got to move because there's no more water here."

Later, my father admitted that, in the confusion of breaking camp, he'd simply forgotten me. He'd been sure that, after a short time, I'd follow of my own accord.

As he lifted me onto his shoulders, I was jubilant, but I bawled.

In the midday heat we caught up with the others.

In the late afternoon, my father sent out a scout. The sun was already setting when the scout returned to report that he had found a place for the night only half an hour away by foot.

Jama and Saïd drove the camels. The scout ran ahead and soon was practically out of sight, swallowed by the reddening earth.

"He's going to purify the ground of evil spirits, and gather wood before it gets too dark," my father explained.

I plodded after him. My skirts wrapped themselves around my legs, making it difficult for me to keep up with the adults' rapid steps.

The spot we reached just as the sun set looked exactly like the one we'd left that morning. In the middle of the steppe, other nomads had already erected fences of thorns, a stall to protect their goats and sheep from night-prowling jackals, hyenas, and wild dogs. They had built huts out of willow branches and woven mats, installed water containers, and placed a fireplace in the center of the space. They had left only a short time ago. Their footprints had not yet been erased by the wind, the animal dung was fresh, the fence intact.

The men began to unpack. Since we'd continue in the morning, the women prepared places to sleep under the stars. Then they began to cook millet for dinner.

After eating, everyone sat around the fire. The adults talked to one another; we children cuddled up together on the mats. I heard my brother say I'd have to sleep on the edge so that when a lion came, he'd get me first, but I was too tired to punch him.

My name is Fadumo Abdi Hersi Farah Husen, the second daughter and fifth child of Mayran Muhammad Elmi and Abdi Hersi Farah Husen. I was born in the Big Rains, 1964. It was a good year: The dry steppes in Ogaden in Somalia, not far from the Ethiopian border, had been green longer than usual, providing nourishment for animals and people alike. Everyone who talks about my birth always mentions the Big Rains.

My oldest brother, Ahmed, already grown up by the time I was born, lived as a soldier in the city. My middle brother, Jama, was eighteen. He was considered the most beautiful in the family because of his muscular physique and even, white teeth. Khadija, my sister, was nine and a stubborn, decidedly temperamental child. She lived mainly in the city with my Uncle Muhammad. From time to time we visited her. My brother Adan was four years old when I was born, and we loved and hated each other. I had stolen his place as the family's little one—just as Muhammad, four years later, would drive me from my mother's arms.

My skin was lighter than all my siblings' and my hair gleamed red under the sun, both signs of beauty in Somalia. My mother, who was small, round, and very dark-skinned, felt very proud of my appearance. She devoted her energy to the family, cooking, caring for the animals, and tilling fields—even during pregnancy. She ground flour, wove rope, produced mats, and cured leather, but she was always ready to spring up to pounce on a naughty child and pull her ears. She was also very strict. My father was a giant with shimmering red hair and a henna-colored beard. A gentle man, he never scolded and only seldom showed anger.

My father fell in love with Mulaho Muhammad Elmi, my mother's sister, but she was already married to my father's uncle. She was very beautiful and songs were sung about her tall frame and long hair. The uncle was old, and when he died, my father asked for Mulaho's hand. But tradition required that she marry the dead husband's brother. In this way, strangers were prevented from marrying, thereby keeping the children in the family.

My father eloped with Mulaho.

They fled, married secretly, and returned only when Mulaho became pregnant. After the birth of my half-sister Halima, the marriage was annulled and Mulaho married the brother of her deceased husband after all. My father was very unhappy about this but eventually married Mulaho's sister, my mother. Because their parents had died when Mulaho and my mother were young, their brothers took on the responsibility of parents. The brothers—my uncles—had wanted the marriages arranged as they had been. When my mother had her first child, she was barely fifteen. Nonetheless, my parents seemed to have a happy marriage; after all, my father was a well-respected man from a good family, and my mother had also inherited the proud character my father had so admired in her sister.

In Somalia we have four major tribes: the Darod, the Dir, the Hawiye, and the Isaaq. The tribes are subdivided into numerous clans that frequently clash. Clan membership has always been very important. Early on, nomadic children learn songs about their clan's history so that even the littlest ones already know clan stories by heart. And often, grandfathers' names go back sixty generations!

I belong to the Darod tribe, Marehan clan, and the family of Reer Kooshin. I have more than a dozen aunts and uncles, about forty cousins, and six half-siblings: I lived with some of them as nomads. My father owned more than fifty camels, more than five hundred sheep and goats, and a dozen cows.

We were a highly respected family.

The moon sank, the women rolled up the mats, the girls drove the goats from the temporary compound, the boys brought the camels, and the men loaded them.

Before dawn the caravan set out.

The sheep milled about in confusion, and the goats ran to any bush that might promise a leaf or two. I followed them on the hard, hot earth, and pierced the soles of my feet on sharp roots while thorn bushes tore at my legs. I carried my shoes in my hands so as not to damage them. Uncle Yusuf and his second wife, Maryan, scolded the children who lagged behind or who had lost a goat. For days we marched from dawn to dusk, covering seemingly endless distances.

On the fifth day Aunt Asha remained seated in the shadow of an acacia. Her huge stomach hurt and she could hardly walk. I didn't understand why no one thought to put her on a camel. The old and the sick weren't expected to walk. Uncle Yusuf explained that the camels were already laden with our huts and equipment and several lambs, so there was no room. My mother set up camp for my aunt and stayed with her. In the evening both women reappeared suddenly out of the darkness. The glow of the campfire illuminated Aunt Asha and the baby in her arms who would be named Iman. She was small and round and snoring. All the girls jumped up and wanted to hold her. Because of the dire need to move on, the next day Aunt Asha tied the baby to her back and walked behind the caravan.

The sky was clear and the landscape changed color with the angle of the sun. Early, we had been bathed in the color of a lion's fur, but toward evening the world was a wild tomato. We passed termite hills meters high: From within came a humming and buzzing, and sometimes I asked myself whether only animals were making these sounds. Why not witches and ghosts? I marveled at the beauty of our animals: the black and white patterns on the goats and the majestic gait of the camels with their long eyelashes decorating languid eyes. Once when I was sick during a move, my father had put me up on a camel. Surrounded by mats, I had lain in the saddle, calmed by the monotonous regularity of the animal's plodding. Soon overcome by fever, I had fallen asleep. I had only awakened as the camel suddenly sprang to one side. My brother Jama had screamed, a whip had struck, and the camel had taken off at a gallop. The men had run after the beast, and it had sped up. It was in overdrive: It flew. And then, suddenly, it had stopped. The saddle, all the goods, and I had flown through the air, landing on a thorn bush. Since then I decided I'd rather walk.

On the afternoon of the ninth day we reached our goal. It was raining, and the earth steamed. Everywhere you looked—green! The trees appeared to shine with an inner radiance; the bushes were fat and luxurious, like rotund sheep. Out of the ground plants shot up that I'd never seen before. The air smelled sweet and our animals were soon full and contented. Aunt Maryan and my cousin Nadifo bent branches into arches and held them in place

9

with sisal cord. My mother unbundled the mats and started to decorate the poles. Before night fell, our huts stood in a half circle with pens for goats and sheep on both outer edges, and all of it surrounded by a fence made of thorn branches. Uncle Yusuf built a fireplace out of stone. My father sprinkled holy water in the four corners of the courtyard and invited the spirits to make their home with us for a while.

Was Mahad okay? Had he made new friends?

Screams echoed through the night, and before I was fully awake, my father rushed into the hut. In the next second he grabbed my brother, turned around, and ran out with him, my mother following with me by the hand. Uncle Yusuf was standing pale as a ghost in front of his hut, and next to him were his wife and the children huddling against her. "Let's go!" shouted my father. "Quick!"

Not understanding what was happening, I stumbled after my mother. She lifted me up, covered my mouth with one hand, and ran through the darkness. Before us was Nadifo. Her older brother Saïd grabbed her. Everyone raced as if lions were after us. As we reached a copse of trees, the adults gagged us and bound our hands together. Someone put me in a leather sack and pulled the cord so that only my head emerged. Men climbed the trees. One of them tied the sack I was in to a high limb. Then the women climbed up and squatted on branches as close to the trunk as they could. My heart beat wildly while, with wide open eyes, I stared into the night.

Coming from somewhere I heard raised voices and angry, raging sounds.

The men ran back. I wanted to call to my father, wanted to know where he was going, wanted to shout, Stay with us! But my mouth produced only a gurgle. "Shush, Fadumo," my mother whispered. "Be still, for Allah's sake!"

Out of fear I peed in my leather sack.

The loud noises approached. I saw burning torches. Someone shrieked. Rigid with fear my family squatted in the trees. My back hurt with terror, a cold, icy pain. I stopped breathing.

At dawn my father returned with the other men. They had driven the attackers away. My father released my gag so that, finally, I could cry. All the children had been stuffed into sacks and hung from branches, so that when we became terrified, as we surely would be, we wouldn't betray the group by making noise when wetting our pants. With shaky legs we stood in front of the trees, and I stared up at my mother, who was still in the branches trying to untie my brother's bundle.

The attackers hadn't escaped with any of our animals, nor had any women or girls in our family been touched. But Uncle Yusuf's second-eldest son had been killed. The other men hadn't been able to save him.

Such attacks were commonplace between tribes, the assault often taking place at night. One of my cousins, who had been dead for many years, had killed many men of the Hawiye tribe—some say as many as four hundred. In revenge the Hawiyes struck us again and again. There was endless bloodshed between the Hawiye and the Darod.

The next day we left our encampment and moved on. Men had tied cloth around the animals' hips so that it swept the ground behind them and wiped out their tracks. Many nights passed before we could sleep peacefully again.

In the morning our camel herder drove the animals to the river a half day's walk away. Later he stood in front of my father, frail, afraid, and grinding his teeth. My father was furious. His favorite camel had separated herself from the herd and disappeared; moreover, the animal was pregnant. My father sent the camel herder out to look for her and then followed. For many days he combed the steppe, looking for tracks, asking other nomads, constantly searching for his camel. Finally, he turned back.

He had never been in such despair.

Weeks passed.

Then a neighbor reported having seen the footprints of a pregnant camel at about two days' walk from our encampment. But a lion had also been on her trail. My father took his dagger, filled a canister with water, and said, "I'll be back soon," before setting off.

For a long time we heard nothing from him.

That is, not until one afternoon, when, not long before sunset, I was returning from herding the goats and ran into a neighbor. The boy, Bile, was my age but I was bigger and, therefore, had beaten him up a number of times. He ran alongside me while keeping some distance, and then shouted suddenly, "Your father has been eaten by a lion!"

Angry, I faced him. "My father's big and strong. No lion would dare to attack him. But your father's so small and ugly, the lions are going to get him!" Then I tore after Bile to beat him up again.

On the way home my stomach felt tied in knots. And as I approached, a terrible sight greeted me: The sand in front of our huts was blood-red. Dead still, my father lay on a mat with his right arm at a strange angle to his body, held on only by a few tendons. His belly spewed blood and intestines. My mother knelt, her clothes blood-soaked. Everywhere—blood, blood, blood, thick, red blood.

A healer came and bound up the wound. Later a holy man recited verses from the Qur'an. My father should only leave this world for another, without pain.

But my father didn't die.

For weeks he lay in our hut, stiff, and nearly paralyzed by pain. His wounds rotted in the heat. Sometimes he lost consciousness to fever. My mother called for his oldest brother, Uncle Yusuf, who was roaming with his herd. It took three weeks for him to arrive. Together with my brother Jama, Uncle Yusuf heaved my father onto his camel and they made their way to the closest town.

Months went by and we heard nothing. We knew neither whether my father was still alive, nor whether he'd found help in the city. We could do nothing but wait until one of my brothers or another relative brought news. We hoped that no news was good news. Had my father died, Uncle Yusuf would have appeared long before to marry my mother. In the meantime, however, we had to move on to search for new pastures.

Half a year later my father returned to us. In the city to which my brother had taken him they had found Chinese construction workers, and among them were doctors who could treat various emergencies. A Chinese surgeon had operated, without anesthesia, placing bands of rubber in my father's elbow so that his arm would have some support as it regained limited motion.

Every day my mother fed my father camel's milk and prepared healing herbs to increase his strength. I massaged his feet. "No one in the family has hands as strong as yours," he praised.

Later my father told us what had happened. He had caught the camel's trail and the day after he set out he had found her near a eucalyptus tree. But he immediately saw that it wasn't his camel after all. The animal had borne its calf. A lion and a lioness then circled around the mother and her young. The male lion had drawn back but the female remained ready to attack. My father resolved to kill her and bring both camels back to camp. He had undone the cloth that served as a turban to protect his head from the sun and wound it tightly around his forearm, from the wrist to the elbow. Then he had drawn his dagger.

But the lion pounced before my father could even throw his weapon. With both paws around him, in a single swift motion, she had ripped open both sides of his body, digging her teeth into his right arm, shredding his flesh, and smashing the bones in his elbow.

My blood ran cold just to hear him tell it.

"I was so desperate that I bit her in the nose with all my strength. That made her let go." Badly wounded, my father had made his way back with the camels. They had walked throughout the entire night and all of the next day until he had reached our huts, where he broke down. I was awestruck.

He laughed. "That lion had the worst bad breath!"

Despite this joke, my father had begun to change. His arm barely moved, the joint almost stiff. He could no longer load up the camels, construct water containers, or chop down trees. He couldn't fight. He was no longer a man. He became known as "one-armed Abdi," the same way they talked about the "four-eyed uncle" who wore glasses. Physical attributes often produced nicknames with us.

My father became withdrawn and silent.

A nomad loves his camels. Without them he can't survive in the steppe. The loss of a camel is worse than the loss of a daughter.

The female camel gives us milk. Camel milk is rich in vitamins, nourishing, and delicious, and often, when stores of water dry up and the next source is many days' walk away, camels' milk is our only food. It quenches thirst and fills you up. Even in the most extreme heat, camels need water only every couple of days; in fact, they can go for a whole month without drinking. This is a good thing, since watering places can be far apart and, during periods of drought, water must be bought at the few spots that provide it. Sometimes a camel herder can stand in line for hours only to find that there's no water left. That signals the time to move on. Male camels are used as beasts of burden: They carry our huts and belongings from one camp to another. They can transport heavy loads and are easy to tame. The females, in contrast, have extremely well-developed memories. They hold grudges and exact revenge.

Men take care of camels; women watch over the goats and sheep. My father, my brothers, and my cousin Saïd knew every single animal in our herd: its character, body, and qualities. Men climb trees to pluck treats for the animals: fruit from the acacia or leaves of the tall eucalyptus. A camel herder will do anything to ensure that his camels are contented.

I also loved our camels. My father possessed one with a single eye, the oldest of all our camels, and my father and he never parted. You had to feed the animal only from the front, never the side, so that he wouldn't take fright. Then he would stretch out his neck and let children climb up before straightening out so that we could slide onto his back and off again. His underhide was sticky with urine, but the smell didn't bother us. It was simply nature. If things got a little too exciting for the cyclops, he would press his legs together, depriving us of air for a second or two before he let us go, and we knew the game was at an end.

I learned to read camel tracks. You can tell from the tracks whether a caravan is loaded; you can even tell to which clan it belongs. You can identify an individual animal by its footprints, know how long ago it had passed by, and whether it was tired. Nomads are as familiar with camels as they are with their immediate families.

A nomad is known by his camels and the size of his herd. Owning many camels means establishing great respect and prestige. Making a present of a camel is the greatest gift Somalis can give.

My cousin Nadifo drove her herd forward. She was big and already circumcised and had permission to take care of the animals all by herself. I had to run to keep up with her and the goats. My favorite goat was called Long-Ear. I had found her as a kid under an incense bush. She had been so tiny she almost starved to death. "Let me relieve the animal of its misery," my mother had said. "It's weak and is going to die anyway." But I had insisted I was going to bring her back to life. With a spoon I had fed her milk that I had gotten from her mother. Now, happily, Long-Ear ran around, following me as if I were her mother, licking my face and nipping at my fingers, wanting to suckle on them.

We ran until we came to a clearing. Nearby was a spring and, in the sand, a pool had formed. We let the animals drink undisturbed. We might not find water again for days. The sun stood high overhead.

"Let's sit in the shade," Nadifo suggested.

We crouched under an acacia and lay down close together on the sand. I was happy to play the wife; Nadifo preferred to be the husband. She giggled, then lowered her voice and made believe she was snoring. "I'm pregnant," I shouted, jumping up. With both hands supporting my back, I stretched out my belly.

"It's no fun to play family when there are only two of us," pouted Nadifo. "We have to be at least five girls." She was right, but I didn't want to stop our game. I was happy to play the mother. ·

"Let's whittle something," Nadifo suggested and pulled off a bit of acacia bark. With nostalgia I rubbed my outstretched belly, then pulled it in, and gave up. Nadifo hummed a tune. She could sing beautifully. We often sang to amuse ourselves, but also to amuse our animals—songs about how the rain would soon come and transform the desert into a flower garden; songs that praised the camels' beauty, comparing them to the women of our tribe. You couldn't give a woman a finer compliment than to compare her beauty to that of a female camel. A woman's neck should be long like a camel's, her hair full like a mane, her movements gracious and elegant, her gait undulating, her eyes dark and mysterious. We sang songs of love and of the life that we would someday lead.

A bird chirped. Some of the goats, nervous now, began to run around. Nadifo jumped up while I grabbed my staff. We ran in opposite directions to drive the animals together and counted them quickly. I looked around—behind every bush there could be a jackal waiting. Jackals crept up silently and ripped a lamb apart without leaving a trace. But if you sprinted screaming in their direction, they'd run away because they were cowards.

In the distance I saw Nadifo wink.

I ran toward her and found a goat in the dust. Next to her was a tiny kid, her skin all wet and sticky. Nadifo knelt down. The goat arched up. Nadifo stroked her neck but the animal screamed. Out of her nether region could be seen protruding the leg of another kid. "Hold on tight," Nadifo soothed, as she slid her hands along the goat's belly and pushed the offending limb back in. Her hand disappeared inside, then her whole forearm. The goat complained. The herd drew back. Hastily, my eyes took in the animals, bushes, grasses. At the same time, I pressed down with all my might, pushing the goat to the ground. I had already helped several times with birthing, especially in the morning while milking. It seemed that the young ones always wanted to enter life feet first so that they had to be turned and helped into the world.

Finally, after four moist little kids lay next to their mother, I rubbed them dry with leaves and gave them names. Then, quick as lightning, I bit off the tips of their left ears. Later, left and right, I would cut slits into their ears with a knife. That was the sign that they belonged to us. They should become as beautiful and tough as Nadifo or as clever and stubborn as I!

The sun was already low in the sky as we made our way home. Long-Ear snapped at my finger. I cuddled her and then shoved her aside. The newborn kids couldn't walk far so I made my scarf into a carrier and laid one inside. On my back, like a mother carrying her children, I carried the young goat home.

From time to time my father would disappear. That wasn't so unusual, although often we didn't know where he was. Sometimes he went to town, sold a pair of sheep and goats, and returned with rice, corn, millet, and cloth. This time he brought back a woman.

My father signaled to her to wait outside the compound. Wrapped in red, she had a thin black and scarlet scarf over her head. She squatted there in the sand. Her skin was very dark. When my mother saw the strange woman, I sensed the air freeze around us. My father unpacked the groceries he had brought. Khadija, home on a visit, opened a sack and let the rice run through her fingers. My father praised its quality. It was especially fine rice. Then he pulled out the presents he had bought. He had never done that before. He displayed colorful fabric with a flowered pattern, a pair of shoes, and aromatic oils. My mother refused even to look at the gifts. Her hand on her hip, her stomach stretched out—she was pregnant again—she walked right past my father and his offerings.

"Come here, Fadumo," he said after a while and winked me over. In his hand was a piece of blue fabric covered with red and yellow flowers. Confused, I looked from my father to my mother and back to my father. I had the feeling I would make a mistake no matter what I did. Then my father stood up, came over to me, and draped the cloth around my shoulders, covering my body. It was exquisite. Outside, beyond the thorn fence, the strange woman sat and looked.

I ran to my mother.

She was chopping wood. Her swollen belly was in the way, but she held it in and hacked at the branches as though she had lost her senses. From time to time her stomach received a dent or two, and the fabric of her wraparound rose and fell. "Why is your stomach moving, Mama?" I asked.

"I ate too much corn," she answered, without looking up.

Later my mother boiled water and prepared corn porridge for the evening meal. Father's gifts were still lying untouched on a mat. My family sat in a circle on the sand, a large wooden plate in the middle. The steaming porridge made my mouth water. Each of us hollowed out a space in the porridge and poured milk and sugar into it. Only my father sat to one side and looked on. My mother offered him neither porridge nor water. I was confused and glanced at Adan and Khadija, trying to read their faces. I felt pulled in two directions. Should I bring my father something to eat? Would my mother slap me?

In silence I ate my porridge.

Later in the evening my parents began fighting. "Take your new wife and get out of here!" my mother shouted. "I have my sons and my daughters. I'm staying. I don't need you."

I was afraid. Uncle Yusuf and the other men would have beaten their wives on the spot had they dared to say anything so disrespectful. My father rose from his stool. I held my breath; my brothers and sisters stood stock still. My mother looked my father in the eyes: fearless, raging, wordless. With every step, my father's body grew more and more powerful. A couple of centimeters in front of my mother he stopped. Like two unequal fighters, they faced each other. Even the goats and sheep were silent. Then my father turned abruptly on his heel and said, "I'm going to move with the children and my new wife to my mother's."

Men travel, and women guard livestock and children. In Somalia, the relationship between the sexes is clearly defined.

A man never does women's work. He takes care of camels, kills lions, and attacks enemy clans. His wife does everything else. Men take themselves seriously, and women treat them as if they are right to do so. Even as small children, girls learn to serve and respect their brothers, fathers, and uncles. A girl rises when a man enters because he might like that precise spot where she has been squatting. Men are always served the best meat, and women the leftovers. Men have their own sleeping quarters, while women and children share mats.

When my father sat with other men, I was proud to bring them tea or to serve a meal. Sometimes he allowed me to sit with him, petted my head, and called me his sunshine. To my father, I was someone special. That the other men wanted to send me away made me angry.

My father was peaceful, just, and respectful of his daughters and women. In a country marked by masculinity, despotism, and violence, my father was a rare man. He expected all family members to fulfill their duties, but he was more considerate, affectionate, and gentle toward children than our mother was, whose constant work left her no time for tenderness.

In Somalia, men enjoy total freedom. They go to town, travel, and maintain more than one wife in various places. A number have several families in many spots, live for months with the first wife and their children, then for a time with the second or third wife and the children he has had with them. If the first wife has borne many sons, the second wife has it hard. But at any time, a man can take a woman's children away. Then she's alone and has nothing.

In Somalia, the world belongs to men.

Long-Ear licked my hand. I stroked her fur between the ears, gave her a kiss, and told her lovingly that she stank but was very beautiful. Then I opened the gate and slid out of the pen. The contented herd had eaten its fill, and you could tell just by looking at the animals that I'd done a good job taking care of them.

In the shadow of a bush my father knelt, facing the East, and prayed. In the courtyard his new wife, Magalo, sat. On a stone next to her stood a bowl and on the fire was a pot. In passing I cast a furtive glance at her. Magalo looked up. I did not speak a word.

Instead I went to my mother, who sat with Uncle Yusuf's second wife, Maryan, in front of her hut. They were both braiding their little daughters' hair. I wanted to cuddle up in my mother's lap, but she pushed me away. My cousin Anisa cried because my mother had found a tick on her head. With a practiced hand my mother loosened the insect and threw it into the fire where it exploded with a muffled thud. Amal, two years older, laughed at her sister for having been so dumb as to get involved with ticks. Anisa gave her a swipe but Amal was quicker, sprang aside, and hopped up and down in the sand before her sister.

"You dirty little thing," Amal called out and laughed. "I'm not playing with you. You're impure." Aunt Maryan scolded, and Amal shut up. Since she'd been circumcised, she boasted and behaved as though she had been a grown-up woman for a long time. Aunt Timiro ground wheat, and the rhythmic thump of the mortar mixed with children's voices, our laughter, and song.

No one paid attention to Magalo.

My father's second wife stood up and went to the water container between our hut and the one right next door that our father had built for her. She moved heavily since she too was pregnant. Aunt Maryan oiled Anisa's braids while my mother disappeared into the hut. I stood up, went to the fire, and threw a handful of sand into the pot with the boiling rice.

A few days later Magalo asked my mother to show her how to prepare the noodles my father had brought back from town. "Throw them into the boiling water and stir," she said, "and whatever you do, don't stop stirring." She hadn't even glanced up from her work. When Magalo poured the noodles onto a wooden plate, nothing but a soft, broken porridge emerged from the pot.

"Yuck!" shouted Adan.

"I'm not eating that," Uncle Yusuf told his first wife. Amal reached for the porridge, grabbed a chunk, held it up, and giggled. Wholly unmoved, my mother bit into a piece of lamb.

I spread the word around that my father's new wife had tried to poison my brother.

Of course I was deaf whenever Magalo tried to talk to me. I ignored her commands, because I wasn't about to put up with anyone replacing my mother, and I showed it.

My mother should have punished me for my naughtiness, but she pretended that nothing had happened. Everyone treated the competition as my mother did: She was invisible to us. A harder punishment doesn't exist. But my mother also ignored my father. Whenever he spoke to her, he might as well have been talking to a tree. Once in a while they fought, loudly and with strength. My father then took to his heels and spent hours in the shade, chewing tobacco and keeping still. Sometimes he chopped twigs, as well as he could with his damaged arm, and made low seats out of them.

Finally he declared the need to move on. Once again the women dismantled the huts, the men herded the camels, the boys helped load them, and the girls kept the goats and sheep together. This time we mapped Somalia's entire length, from Ogaden at the Ethiopian border to the north where my father's family lived. The trip was oppressive. The heat spread over animals and people like a blanket, making them sweat and slowly dry up. From day to day, my mother grew weaker, but she let nothing show. Sometimes I slipped her a few berries or roots I had found under a bush.

The closer we got to the north, the more mountainous the landscape became. High plateaus replaced flat steppes. At some point, when we reached the foothills, the men herded the camels together. Uncle Yusuf declared a pause. The women poured water into cups and gave everyone a drink.

Then we began the ascent.

In single file the camels plodded up the pass, over tiny trails and sharp rocks, always following the leader. Jama and Saïd had bound them together, the reins tied to the tail of one and the halter of the next. Nadifo and I rounded up a goat that had broken away from the herd. Our feet were bleeding. The higher we climbed, the deeper the chasms. The massive cliffs were seemingly piled one on top of the other by some arbitrary hand. I was so overpowered by the view, and at the same time so concentrated on driving the goats forward, that I jumped as sudden shrieks pierced the air.

A female camel had fallen into the abyss!

Stuck between two promontories the animal lay, one leg pressed to its chest, the other squashed behind its back, its skull drenched in blood. Everywhere were scattered mats and pots, cooking utensils and canisters. My father and Uncle Yusuf's sons were using all their energy to maneuver the other animals past the site, but they resisted, stubbornly refusing to move forward or back. Shouts and hysterical voices echoed from cliff to cliff, and always the victim's groans. The women began to blindfold the herd in order to lead them past the wounded beast. Saïd, Jama, and Uncle Yusuf moved carefully down the crag to kill the unfortunate creature and bring back whatever could be saved of our possessions. Around the fire that evening I saw tears in Uncle Yusuf's eyes. My father and Saïd were also moved.

Weeks later we reached a river weaving through the landscape like a narrow band of cloth. Water rippled, slapping the shore, gurgling and licking at the lichens growing on either side. Never in my life had I seen so much water in one place. I ran along the bank. Behind me I heard my mother call out as she followed, gesturing hysterically: "Watch out for the crocodiles!"

"What's a crocodile?" I asked.

Soon the camels were relieved of their burdens, and Jama and Saïd led them to the river to drink. Nadifo and I herded the goats and sheep a short distance further upstream. I listened to the sounds of their mouths, the slurping of tongues and lips. Again and again I knelt at the edge as well, dipped water with both hands, let it run down my body, my neck, my arms, my face. It was cool and fresh and smelled sweet. I dipped and dipped without stopping, drank and drank, trying to swallow so much water that I'd never feel thirsty again. Never again did I want to feel dryness split my lips, crack my neck, or slow my tongue, making swallowing difficult. I drank until my stomach was full and then I sank, groaning, to the ground. Through my clothes I felt the cool dampness of the earth.

The animals, too, were happy to have their stomachs full, and we children turned to play. Saïd taught me to walk on my hands. He let me do cartwheels and bounce on his knees. From the white sand we built little huts with courtyards and campsites, then shaped pottery of clay and filled it with water. We clowned around, each acting out a scene: "My Father Has the Most Magnificent Camels; My Brothers Are the Greatest!" We threw ourselves into the mud and splashed as we'd never done in any puddle before. I massaged my feet and dipped them in water, letting the blisters and wounds cool. I was happy to stop walking. With Nadifo and my other cousins, I played family. Sometimes I was the man and beat my wife; then I was the wife and the wind blew a baby into my tummy. I sneezed three times, and it was born.

The men started building a raft. They felled branches from the surrounding trees and bound them with sisal cord. As the float neared completion—approximately one meter in width and in length—Jama took it into the water. Again, the camels were blindfolded as they had become obstinate and bellowed as soon as the men tried to lead them to the raft. The rocking movement frightened them, and they shied and bucked. With rods and calls, with shouts and tender petting, the men finally heaved one animal after another onto the raft. To calm the camels, they sang. Jama crooned while leading his favorite camel: "As long as I live, and am not yet underground, I'll know the meaning of your beauty. . . ."

Many days passed while the whole herd was being transported. Freed from nearly all duties, I played and watched the goats and camels sitting contentedly in the sand, chewing leaves with their elongated jaws, from the middle to the right, from the right to the middle, from the middle to the left, chomping with always the same movement that made me feel so at home.

The animals remained upstream at a bend in the river, accompanied by Saïd and a camel boy. The rest of us went on to the nearby village.

I had never seen a village before.

We reached a collection of courtyards. They looked like the ones we had set up on the steppes, except that the people here made their homes not of willow branches and mats, but of stone. My oldest brother, Ahmed, had once told us about a town when he came back on a visit. He had reported that he had also seen animals made of metal: They didn't eat or sleep, but stank and shrieked and had round legs. They were called cars. I hadn't believed a word.

Curious, I approached one of the stone huts. The door was open, so I went inside. It was dark and suddenly I could no longer hear the wind. Afraid, I ran out. A sound—a shrill howl—forced me to hold still. Something was bearing down on me, then came a screech, and my heart stood still. Adan threw me to the side, I tripped and fell and a stinking metal animal zoomed by. When I stood, my back hurt from fear, my legs wouldn't behave, and my feet had gone numb. Rigid, I stared after the car. So Ahmed hadn't lied.

Village life was dangerous.

My father led us to the home of a distant aunt. She also lived in a stone hut surrounded by a stone wall. What fascinated me were the multicolored slivers of glass embedded on top of the ledge. In the steppe, from time to time, I had found pieces of glass and kept them in my collection of treasures. These glass bits were not only beautiful, but useful. You could use them for cutting if you forgot your knife; you could use them to make a fire if you forgot your matches; and they colored the world in radiance and mystery if you held them before your eyes. I wanted to touch these pretty glass stones, so I climbed up the wall. A second after reaching the top, I sliced my hand.

The village children laughed.

They laughed again as my aunt offered me a banana. Never having seen the fruit before, I bit into it without removing the skin and spat it right out. They laughed once more when I refused to use the outhouse. In the steppe you simply disappeared behind a bush, and here I was supposed to squat over a stinky, slippery hole in a dark wooden shack. The village children owned toys that I'd never seen before. They ate vegetables with gravy. They acted as though all that I knew nothing about was unbelievably significant. Since I'd never seen my grandmother before and all the children I knew had grandmothers, I couldn't wait to meet mine. I encountered a morose woman, small, wrinkled as a berry, wearing a stained wraparound. She shuffled grumbling through the courtyard, speaking a dialect I could not understand. Nor could she understand me. When I was sure that no one could overhear, I asked my mother why grandma had no pointer finger on her left hand.

"She chopped it off because she had been promised to an old man she didn't want to marry. With a mutilated hand, a woman is worthless, so the old man decided to do without her. Later grandma married grandpa. He couldn't have cared less how many fingers his wife had."

After a while my father apologized to my mother and gave her a camel. A few days later, my mother gave birth to my brother Muhammad. Magalo also had a boy. But shortly thereafter she disappeared, and we never saw her again. My family also left my grandmother's house to return to the steppe.

After the birth of a child, a nomadic woman is well cared for. For forty days she never leaves her hut. Her sisters, sisters-in-law, cousins, and women neighbors bring her food and drink, providing her with everything she needs. This is the only time that a nomadic woman takes leave from her otherwise hard life.

Once the forty days have passed, the baby's hair is cut, and he or she receives a name, becoming a real member of the family. Children in Somalia are considered a gift from God. If the child— and especially the first born—is a boy, joy overflows. Everyone shouts, "Hooray and what good fortune! My brother (or sister or son or cousin) has just had a boy!" The stature of a father and mother increases with the birth of a son. Even I—a girl—gained status because I had four brothers.

If the baby is a girl, the family looks forward to having another worker. I was hardly bigger than a goat myself when I was sent to herd the flock. I learned to make cord, baskets, and containers, to weave the mats on which we slept and from which we built our huts, to make flour and butter, to milk. By age seven, if not sooner, a nomadic girl can take charge of an entire household. And as soon as she is circumcised, she is allowed to slaughter goats or bring her father the ritual water before he prays.

My mother was always pregnant. She had a number of miscarriages, and those babies whom she did give birth to did not always survive. Somalis interpret the death of a baby as they do everything else in life, as the will of God.

The teacher was dressed in white, his hair was parted down the middle, and his beard reached to his chest. Today he was in a bad mood. That's why he let us sweat under the sun while he sat cross-legged under the shade of a tree. From a container he poured water into a bowl. Reverently he held it in his hands, gazed at it, murmured a few words, brought it to his well-padded, bulging lips, took a swallow, and passed it to the oldest boy.

This ritual signaled the start of our lessons each morning.

Qur'anic school was the only school far and wide, and my father had made up his mind that Adan would attend. I begged and pleaded, wanting desperately to go to school too. "You're a curious one," my mother decided. "Go with your brother." The following week, when the teacher reappeared, I simply walked in behind Adan. In the meantime Nadifo guarded my goats.

All the pupils brought small wooden tablets that were so brightly polished that they shone in the sun. My father had whittled my tablet small and light like me. The teacher poured powdered coal into a dish and added goat milk. The longer he stirred it with his finger, the pastier it got. Once it reached the right consistency, he dipped a stick the size of a finger into the mixture and began to draw a flourish from right to left, with flowing movements.

"That is a letter," said the teacher and held up the board.

I saw a wavy line with a lot of dots on top, moving all the way across.

"Letters make up words, words become sentences, and sentences become texts. The verses in the Qur'an are texts. You will be able to read the holy book later on. We will learn to write."

I had no idea what he was talking about. I had never seen a book. Stories were told; no one had to read or write in order to learn to recite them.

With my left hand, I held my board the way I had been shown and started to copy the letters. My movements were awkward and the pasty ink dried faster than I could write. A boy made fun of me. The teacher pulled his ear and the boy started to cry.

"Lick your board clean," the teacher said. "Lick it clean and swallow so you'll have no more evil thoughts in you."

We children didn't like the teacher. We discovered that when he spoke, small drops of saliva spewed from his mouth. Like shiny pearls they shot through the air. You saw them clearly if you sat in a particular corner. At first I was fascinated by the saliva. But I soon realized that this spit also landed in the holy water that he gave us every morning to drink.

"You evil child! Drink the water," he shouted, angered by my rebellion.

"No."

"Drink!" he screamed. His rod hit my thigh.

"No. You spit in the water. That's disgusting."

A second slash burned my arm.

I took my board and hit him back.

The switch sliced through the air, hitting my arm, my head, my back. I stumbled over the other children, ran, flew out of there. I heard the teacher call after me, "I never want to see you in my school again!"

At home my mother scolded me. "You naughty girl! You've shamed me. I'll end up in hell because I have brought up such a bad daughter!" I cried because of my guilty conscience but also from rage. What had I done wrong?

I took my sandals, a cup, and a mat and bound it all together in some cloth. "You're mean. I'm running away!" Angry, I threw the bundle over my shoulder and stomped to the door.

My mother looked at me. Suddenly she started to laugh. "I believe you would."

"I'm going to Mahad's." After all, his mother was my aunt.

"So you know where they live?"

"I'll find out," I called and marched out.

I didn't get far, and once back home, I was still angry that girls had to obey.

A thousand stings like pricks from tiny thorns—on my feet, legs, arms, back, stomach, and head. Yes, the stings on and in my head were the worst. They never stopped, not by day or night. I prayed that sleep would deliver me, but Allah didn't listen. In the morning, when my mother gave us three or four spoonfuls of water mixed with a little milk to drink, the stinging abated. But scarcely had my body absorbed the liquid than the pain began again, more insistent than ever. My eyes burned, and all movement hurt.

I imagined the river. I saw water, endless amounts of water, still fresh, and could feel the cool air. I let the water flow over my hands and run through my fingers. I scooped the water with both hands and drank, greedily.

I woke up. Sand stuck to my lips. On my tongue. On my gums. Sand, everywhere. I stared at my fingers; my hands—they were clawing the hot dune. The dream had dissolved. I coughed. I spit.

I was thirsty. For weeks now I had known nothing but thirst.

My brother Muhammad lay under a tree. His small chest rose and fell, barely perceptible. He was unconscious. My mother, her eyes bulging in her emaciated skull, noticed him and did a double take. She had been unable to feed him. She dug a hole in the earth and buried him up to his neck, hoping to delay his drying out, to seal in whatever remaining moisture he still had in his little body.

It was the worst drought in ages. Everywhere you could smell the rot of goats, sheep, and cows dead in their pens. Even the camels were nothing but skin and bones. My father looked for water. He had already been on the trail for many days. Even though I was little, I went with the women to fetch water, but they walked so quickly and

I was already too weak, too frail—as thin as a finger. And every time we had to go farther, and farther. Anyone who owned a spring had stopped selling water to enemy clans long ago. The drought had lasted too long already, and nobody knew when it would end. Fights broke out; people battled over the precious liquid.

My tongue was thick and heavy: a furry foreign animal that filled my mouth and took away my breath.

We lay in the half shade of trees.

Waiting.

Shriveling.

The man had brought two cows, rice, wheat flour, coffee, and sugar. Oil for my mother. Fabric for Khadija. Sandals for me. Uncle Yusuf's first wife slaughtered a sheep. My mother and Uncle Yusuf's second wife prepared the evening meal, grinding corn and gathering nuts. The men sat under an acacia, smoking, drinking tea, and chatting. I asked my mother why I couldn't join them. "They're discussing important things," she answered. "Besides, you're a girl."

I ran to Khadija. My sister sat in our hut with long, thin grass-es on her knees. The thick weave would soon become a bowl. Then she'd put herbs in it and rub them into the heated strands to seal it. Later, when my mother filled the bowl, the aroma of herbs would perfume the milk. Khadija's movements were deft and strong. I asked why she was angry. She waved me away. "You're too little to understand."

"I'm about to be circumcised," I retorted. "Then I'll be grown up like you."

My sister stared at me as though she had never seen me before. I figured I wasn't going to get any answer, but suddenly, Khadija threw the half-finished bowl into the corner and exclaimed, "I'm NOT going to marry that old man!"

My breath stuck in my throat. "You're getting married?"

"NO! I'd rather feed myself to the lions."

I shivered and besieged my sister. She should tell me everything.

But she was so angry that I had to beg for every word. It took a while for me to understand that my Uncle Muhammad had decided to marry off my sister. Our father had agreed. I nearly burst from excitement and ran out. I couldn't understand why Khadija refused to get married. Every girl dreamed of her wedding day and all the presents. The men were still sitting under the acacia. They drank tea and haggled. Out of the corners of their mouths dribbled the juice of chewing tobacco. From a distance I observed the foreigner. He was really old. Older than my father. A grandfather. He also limped—I had noticed that when he arrived. We children clowned after him, imitating his walk. Adan said it was a war wound, but was he telling the truth? How did Adan know?

I ran to my mother for permission to bring the men fresh tea.

She looked at me. "You're curious, Fadumo," she said. "And cheeky! You know you're not supposed to disturb the men."

I hid behind an incense bush. After a while the old man stood up. Stiff and awkward, his wounded leg dragged behind as if it belonged to somebody else. Scarcely had the guest retreated than I ran to my father, grabbed the teapot, and promised to bring a fresh brew.

In a whisper, Uncle Muhammad called my father a knuckle-head. "For Khadija, you can get at least twenty camels. She's a very beautiful girl from a good family." With his own daughters Uncle Muhammad had had no luck. One was too short, the second not very pretty, and the third still a little child whom he could promise to someone but only marry off years later.

My father spit a wad of tobacco into the sand. His face was impossible to read: "My daughters shouldn't think I would auction them off."

"You're not only a knucklehead, you're crazy!" scolded Uncle Muhammad. "Twenty camels! Plus a rifle, a horse, and groceries. Just think of all the presents!"

My father shook his head and broke off a fresh chunk of tobacco.

Bewitched, I stood there frozen, the teapot in my hand.

The next day the old man mounted his horse and left. With the help of a cousin, Khadija had run away to town, and Saïd swore to shoot the old geezer if he should as much as look at our sister again.

Eighty-two, eighty-three, eighty-four.

I started again. The result was the same.

One was missing.

I counted and counted, but no matter how often I did it, one goat had disappeared without my noticing. Anxious and on wobbly legs I made my way toward home.

"You're irresponsible," my father scolded as I drove the animals into their pen. He threw bark at me, hitting my heel. "Run and find your goat!"

Crying, I ran back. Tears blinded me so that I scarcely recognized the trail. I simply sprinted toward the myrrh where I had brought the herd that morning. Soon night fell. I sought a tree, an acacia, anything by which to orient myself. But everything sank further and further into the darkness of night. In the distance I heard a muffled rumble. I was afraid. Carefully, I felt my way. The air smelled fresh, and suddenly I understood what was announcing itself: thunder. A storm was coming. The next moment lightning revealed the landscape. Blinded by the flash, I shut my eyes. Then, behind my pupils, an image formed. A eucalyptus tree had been there. I changed direction. After the rain, animals would leave their lairs. And I could already hear hyenas and a lion.

I ran faster.

Two sharp strokes of lightning blazed across the sky. Only a couple of hundred meters separated me from the eucalyptus. What I failed to see was the bush. Without warning I tripped on a branch, screamed, and landed in the thorns. Paying no attention to the pain, I swung my rod in all directions; if there had been an animal sheltering there, I had to chase it off before it got me.

But I was alone.

With the rod I pushed aside the offending branches to form a cradle. In the dark I felt for the thorns in my feet, legs, arms, and hands to pull them out. A heavy rainfall began. The drops were so big that they hurt my skin. Again the lightning turned night to day. Only a few feet away I spied a tree stump. The next moment, in the darkness, it resembled an animal. It seemed to be moving. I pulled my dress more tightly around me, prayed to Allah, and asked all good spirits to let me wake up in the morning in peace.

All around me animals shrieked.

As the first light invaded the horizon, I looked around. I had no idea where I was, so I crawled out of the bush and simply walked in circles, for hours, always stumbling across my own tracks. I panicked. I was thirsty and hungry. My wounds hurt. I saw lion tracks and evidence of a hyena in the sand.

I was especially fearful of hyenas. They would lie patiently, waiting for their victim to become exhausted. Only then would they dare to attack. I heard barking. Very aggressive, wild dogs always show up in packs.

I jumped at every noise, fearful of anything that moved.

As the sun set, I climbed a tree, undid my dress, wrapped it around a branch and tied myself tight. I ate berries, a root, and leaves. The leaves would keep me full for a while, but I hadn't found much else to eat. My bladder was killing me but I knew that as soon as I let go of a drop, wild animals would be on my trail. Despite knowing that, it was urgent. I had to climb down and relieve myself. I grabbed the stones I'd brought up with me and threw them down, screaming. Whatever might be lying in wait at the trunk had to be driven away. But nothing stirred. Carefully I descended, ran over the steppe, squatted behind a bush, and sprinted back. Once up on the branch, I tied myself to it again, so that if I fell asleep, I wouldn't fall. And it wasn't long before a pack of hyenas settled at the foot of my perch. My heart beat so loudly that I was afraid they would hear it.

The whole night I sweated without budging.

At dawn, the hyenas left.

Every morning on waking I'd untie my dress, climb down, and run. For hours I simply stumbled around. I cried, called out for my mother, whimpered. Why wasn't she there to help me? Why didn't she hear me? Why didn't anybody come for me? I was afraid but also ashamed. My father had just returned from a trip and had brought me a beautiful piece of fabric. I wanted to prove what a big girl I was and, instead, I had lost a goat. This was just like the time when a leopard followed me.

Leopards are fast and good climbers, so hiding in trees is of no use. I had thrown a stone and had driven him off. But he'd already broken the neck of one of my goats. Crying, I had kneeled next to the body.

Now I ate roots and looked for berries.

I found an ostrich nest and stole an egg, but the male bird attacked me. I ran and threw myself into a thornbush where the needles pierced my flesh.

I ate a poisoned berry. In seconds my tongue was swollen and hardly fit in my mouth. I found wild garlic and a floral anesthetic to help my stomachache.

When it rained, I caught the drops in large leaves, or I spread out my cloth and wrung the water out into my mouth. I made straws out of grasses and used them to suck up the moisture from the little holes in branches. The earth, drenched with rain, smelled sweet. It was soft and gentle under my feet. The air cooled. As much as I longed for such days throughout the year, I couldn't enjoy them then. In despair and overcome with terror, every evening I climbed a tree and tied myself tight.

Then, one morning, I heard the complaints of a goat and the bleating of sheep. Quick as the wind I untied myself, climbed down the tree and ran as fast as I could in the direction of the herd. My cousin Nadifo gestured wildly as she recognized me. Soon my father came running, then my mother and sisters and brothers. For days I had been not far from them at all, but didn't know it. They had been desperate to find me but the rain had washed away my tracks. My mother gave me a big hug, and my father lifted me onto his shoulders and carried me home.

I was cared for and spoiled. They pulled the thorns out of my wounds, massaged my feet and oiled my skin so it would heal. Everyone was jubilant to see that I'd survived. Nobody said a word about the missing goat.

After I'd recovered, my parents conferred on me responsibility for the entire herd. I had lost one animal but I'd also proven that I could survive in the wild. "Now," said my father, "you're grown up."

The ululation could be heard from afar. I ran out of the hut, the sun blinding me for a moment. My mother whipped across the courtyard, balling her wraparound in her fist so she could move more freely, and raced toward the man. At first I didn't recognize him because he wore his hair short and looked too thin. My mother laughed, letting her tongue click against her palette, and let go with the typical ululation of Somali women—the sign of joy. "Ahmed! My firstborn son is back! Thanks be to Allah!"

Frozen, I stood in the shadow of the hut, still dirty from herding the goats, and watched how my mother hugged my brother, stroked his face, and kissed his hands. Then I, too, ran to Ahmed.

My mother started to prepare a festive meal and all the other women pitched in. I swept the courtyard and spread mats. Jama hurried over and joined my father, Adan, and Uncle Yusuf, in pelting Ahmed with questions: What path had he taken? Had he been attacked? How were our uncle, cousins, brothers, and sisters in the city? Everyone shouted at once, claimed the right to sit next to the guest, and passed drinks. My mother served camel milk. Everyone celebrated Ahmed's return.

My brother had brought gifts and to my surprise and delight, most were for me: fabric in the prettiest colors; a pearl necklace, shining yellow; blue plastic sandals with buckles—ones I had wanted for a long time. The leather sandals my father made from time to time had begun to squeak, had become wet, and were disintegrating even before the animals had nibbled on their soles. But the most fascinating present was a collapsible pocket mirror. I had seen something similar only once before in my life, at my aunt's in the city. Carefully I pressed my thumb against the narrow plastic button.

The mirror sprang open. I saw a face.

It was strangely large and distorted.

Laughing, I closed the mirror, shook myself, opened it again, and looked. Khadija pulled my arm, and a hundred hands reached at the same time for the pocket mirror. All the girls pushed and wanted to see what this was all about. I felt like a queen. I hugged my brother and drowned him in kisses. "Thank you, Ahmed."

Ahmed picked me up and tossed me in the air until I got dizzy. He was the best brother in the world. If I had my way, I'd marry him. My mother stood next to us. "Your brother has come for your sake," she said and petted my hair. I didn't understand what she meant but I felt like the most important person in the universe.

"You've really gotten big," he said.

Dusk had fallen as my family gathered in the courtyard. We sat cross-legged in front of our huts. The fried goat smelled and tasted wonderful. I snuggled up to my mother and envied little Muhammad who, courageously, cavorted about under Ahmed's legs. Everyone ate and laughed and described what had happened since Ahmed's last visit.

Later, when I was alone, I took out my presents. Carefully I draped the fabric around my body, veiled my head, twisted and turned, put on the pearls, slipped into the plastic sandals and examined my feet. Everything smelled so new and promising. I closed my eyes and breathed the aroma so as to remember it always. Then I opened the buckle on the sandals, undid the pearls, and folded the fabric. The pearls and the shoes I gave to my mother, who locked them in a trunk. The cloth I placed on the mats. At night I'd use it as an aromatic pillow.

"Tomorrow's your big day," my mother said.

Khadija said, "If you die, I'll get your presents."

My skin crawled as if there were ants all over it. I heard mother's breath, my brothers' snores, the goat's and sheep's baying. Before going to bed my mother had bathed me, scrubbing my body with soap, and cut my finger- and toenails. She had braided my hair and rubbed my body with buttermilk so that I smelled like perfume.

I'm going to be married, I thought. Then I realized that I couldn't marry. I was still impure.

Is that what my mother had meant?

I was seven years old. Before the last Big Rains almost all the girls my age had had *gudniin*, circumcision. But I had been sick. The child will die, my mother had objected. She had not permitted them to come for me. Aunt Asha hadn't allowed my cousin Iman to be circumcised either. A bird shrieked. I felt mother's breath on my neck. On this night Muhammad had to give up his accustomed spot. For the first time since I was a baby I was privileged to lie in my mother's arms. But I couldn't sleep. My stomach felt hot and hollow. All girls anxiously await their circumcision, but nobody talks about it. I thought of Nadifo and Amal. They had boasted and spread the word that they were beautiful and pure, and the rest of us were dirty. But sometimes I'd see a girl coming back home crying. Some girls became ill. Whatever lay before me, I knew it was going to be painful.

If only the excisor would die, this very night!

I was shocked at my own thoughts. Excisors are believed to have magical powers. There was something mysterious about them. What would happen should she detect my evil wish? With what spirits was she on intimate terms? Quickly I mumbled a few words of apology, pleaded with the spirits, and wished her a good long life.

It was still dark when my mother woke me. She told me to be quiet. Quickly I stood up, pulled my cloth around me, and followed her. The air was clear and cool, a bird warbled, and the cacophony of voices from the night before—the singing and laughter—still echoed in my ears.

My mother carried a water bottle and a tub. The tub was very big, large enough to sit in. But I didn't want to know what we would use it for. Instead I concentrated on the sound of our footsteps: four feet moving quickly over hardened sand. With every meter that moved us further from our encampment, my fear grew.

36

My heart banged against my ribs. I was nauseated. I felt as though my stomach had become unhinged. I felt my mother's eyes on me. I couldn't run away. Her hand clamped mine.

Finally we reached a wide bare clearing. A single acacia stood at its edge. The light turned brown, then gray, and the brighter it got, the more the landscape lost its beauty for me. Out of the darkness thorn bushes, dried plants, and cracked soil emerged. "We'll wait here," my mother said and squatted in the sand.

"Where are Aunt Asha and Iman?"

"They're coming later."

Wordlessly, we sat next to each other. The stillness was frightening. It announced mischief and made me realize my powerlessness with every second that elapsed. I was afraid I'd throw up.

"Look," said my mother, getting up and going to the acacia. "Look what we've prepared for you and your cousin." Someone had pulled the branches of the tree to meet the earth, creating a kind of hut. Along the sides thorns had been placed to ward off wild animals. The floor had been stamped smooth and covered with mats.

A camp. For an unknown period of time.

Although the sun was still low, I began to sweat.

At the other end of the clearing a figure appeared. The woman looked ancient and she walked with a stoop. Despite appearances, she advanced rapidly toward us. When she reached us, my mother welcomed her with respect. The old woman mumbled a couple of words I didn't understand and, without casting even a glance at me, sat down. She was wearing a dirty, torn wraparound, and her skin was wrinkled. She spread out a cloth in the dust and began reciting a secret spell to ward off evil spirits and the devil.

A witch. She was most certainly a witch.

The old woman began to empty a pouch and spread out her utensils: a little sack of ash, a rod, a small metal container with herbal paste, thorns from a bush, and elephant hair. She broke a razor blade into two halves. Her lids hung heavy over both eyes, and I asked myself whether she could see what she was doing. She

37

grasped the rod, trimmed the top end, and slipped the razor blade into a slit. Then she wrapped sisal cord around the instrument. It looked like a little ax.

I wanted to scream. I wanted to run away.

But I didn't want to bring shame on my family.

Nervously I plucked at my arms. My skin felt hot and had gone numb. What were they were going to cut out of me? My mother put her arms around my shoulders. The old woman still had not looked at me.

"Sit down," she murmured, and gestured with her thumb toward the tub that my mother had placed upside down in the sand.

"Sit on it," my mother said.

My heart was racing. My mouth was dry and not a word came out. I sat on the tub. My mother squatted behind me and held me tight. A hand shoved my skirt up. Suddenly I heard Aunt Asha's voice. She said that I should raise my legs and put my feet, left and right, on the tub's rim. Hands touched my body everywhere, a horde of hands, pressing, tearing, pulling. A voice said: "Hold her tight!" A hand gagged my mouth.

The first cut was ice cold.

A deep blue pain.

A lightning bolt to the head.

The voice of my mother, calling: "Don't scream like that. Don't shame me. Be a big girl!"

This *cold*.

Blood on my backside, ice cold blood.

I bucked under an all-consuming, devouring pain.

A shriek to the ends of the world wanted to escape but stuck in my throat. It couldn't get out.

The world stopped spinning. Everything went numb.

And soft.

Oh, so soft and light and beautiful. A cocoon of fine sand, taking my body up and carrying me off, hugging me, protecting me.

When I came to, I felt nothing. I heard scraping, scratching noises, and voices. I was floating and looking on from overhead, seeing myself on the ground, on the upside-down tub, stiff as a board, my mother and Aunt Asha holding me tight, putting a block of wood in my mouth, and an old woman squatting between my legs, carrying out her barbaric craft.

At some point I could breathe again. I screamed: "Mommy, help me!"

But it didn't stop. It didn't stop for a very long time.

2

Salt water washed the wound. The old woman took a fistful of thorns, sharpened them with her blade so they'd pierce the skin more easily, and began to sew me. I tried to defend myself but strong hands still pressed me down.

"Hold still. It will soon be over," my mother said. "You're not the first to go through this."

I cried. I could hear the thorns squeal as the old woman pushed them through my skin. One broke off and she spent an eternity trying to dig out the end caught in my flesh.

I became the agony, the cold as ice agony, in my spine.

When I awoke the next day, my whole body ached. Although I was aware of every limb, none seemed to belong to me. They had separated us—my body and me. We were no longer a whole.

Softly I called my mother. She called for the excisor. Together they carried me to a corner of the hut, lay me down on the sand, turned me on my side and drew my legs up to the appropriate angle. The excisor squatted behind me. I tried to urinate.

But it was impossible.

"Pull yourself together," murmured the witch. "Try harder." With her palm she hit my thigh. Fire raced down my leg.

"Bite my arm," my mother said. "I know it hurts." But still not a drop emerged. The excisor began fumbling with my bandage. At every touch I panicked.

"The child is all sewn up," I heard my shocked mother exclaim. "She'll die like that!"

The excisor complained and cursed and spit in the sand. With cold fingers she pulled a thorn out of my flesh. It squealed.

"But don't open her too wide," my mother called. The old woman slurred something unintelligible. It took half an hour to empty my bladder. The urine burned the open wound; tears ran down my face. Then the old woman replaced the bandage from hip to knee. Thorns bit into my thighs.

"Now you're a clean girl," my mother said and stroked my cheek. "You'll glow. You'll shine."

Somalis have their daughters circumcised to make them beautiful and clean. It's an ancient tradition.

The girls can't wait for this big day. But they don't know what they're waiting for. The custom is widespread, yet no one talks about sex at all. Afterward, the girls know only that they have become women.

Excisors remove the clitoris and labia minora. Sometimes they scrape the inside of the labia majora and remove tissue from the vagina. They use razor blades, slivers of glass, knives, scissors, and sometimes even their sharp fingernails. Then they sew the outer lips with thorns and thread so they adhere. Only a minuscule opening remains for urine and menstrual blood to exit drop by drop.

Female genital mutilation takes place in many African countries, in Asia, even in the United States and Europe, but the rites differ considerably. A few have only the clitoral foreskin removed, and they aren't sewn. In Somalia, however, 98 percent of girls are subjected to *gudniin*, or infibulation, as I was.

Tradition is powerful. It's unthinkable to work against tradition. No girl would want to avoid circumcision, for it would mean exclusion. Somalis assume that their religion sanctions circumcision, but people of different faiths perform it as well. It's considered hygienic and aesthetic, since female genitalia must be cut and sewn before they can be considered beautiful. In addition, infibulation ensures girls' chastity, or so it is thought.

My operation cost a good number of goats. Most excisors in Somalia belong to a tribe that is not highly respected but that charges a lot for their services. The circumcision of girls is a lucrative business.

According to the World Health Organization's estimates, 140 million women have been circumcised, and each year 2 million more endure the procedure. The consequences for the health of girls are horrendous. Girls die from shock or loss of blood; they experience infections; they wind up with chronic ailments; they lose their fertility. And they suffer for life as a result of the trauma. All of that is known and nonetheless . . .

It's an ancient tradition.

Only a few hours after the excisor removed the thorns, I came down with a fever. Heat crept up my legs and into my stomach. Blood and flesh pulsated and bubbled, knocking with such force that I thought my body was going to explode. Make it stop! I wanted to scream and rip off the bindings on my legs. Air, I longed for cooler air! Next to me lay my cousin Iman, silent and still, tears running down her cheeks.

Then I fell asleep.

I awoke to find my mother kneeling beside me. Carefully, she helped me turn from one side to the other. Lying on my stomach or flat on my back was impossible. She offered me berries and goat's milk; I accepted the berries but not the milk. The stink of pus and rotting flesh began to spread. I tugged on the bindings, but my mother shoved my fingers aside. I felt as if I were being boiled alive with the heat and the pounding, the hammering inside me, the swelling ever louder—roaring. My face burned.

Hellfire. Everywhere.

When I came to, my tongue stuck to my gums. My lips were

42

dry and my eyes burned. My skull felt as if I were hanging upside down from a tree. "My child . . ." said my mother. Her glance directed inward, she looked very sad. I extended my hand. My mother held my fingers, kissed them, and stroked my face. She jumped up and gave me water. Greedily I drank, feeling every swallow run down my throat. Through the ceiling seeped muted afternoon sun. I heard a bird trill and, in the distance, the clucking of a camel herd. The spicy aroma of dust, earth, and weeds penetrated the hut. The other side of the mat, on which both I and my cousin Iman had lain, was empty.

Later my mother told me that, while I was unconscious, she had sat watching over me for seven days and nights. Drop by drop she had given me water, had placed cool cloths on my forehead and fanned the fresh air around me. She had prayed. And then she had ordered my shroud and called an *imam*—the prayer leader, but he had refused to bless me because men are forbidden to approach circumcised girls. My mother, however, insisted, for she wanted me to appear pure before God when I died. At last, the *iman* sprinkled holy water over me and recited a couple of verses from the Qur'an.

"Mommy," I said. "Mommy, I'm so hungry." My mother broke into laughter, laughed and cried. She thanked Allah and projected a shrill ululation that soon brought all the women and girls in our family to rejoice and celebrate that I was alive.

They slaughtered a sheep and enjoyed a big feast.

Three weeks passed before the remaining thorns could be removed. Iman recovered quickly but I felt ill. The wound continued to pulsate, but a bit less painfully, and the twitching had become a knocking—a sleeping animal not to be trusted. Again, my legs were bound, though not so tightly this time. Still, I could take only tiny steps. But I didn't want to move. I was afraid to.

I felt wiped out, shrunken, worthless. My energy had evaporated. Instead, fear and mourning ruled my body. "You've changed," my father remarked. "What's the matter with you?"

I didn't have words with which to answer him.

I spent my days in the hut, working obediently on the tasks assigned to me. I wove bowls and baskets; I was silent and conscientious. Outside, I could hear girls running around and driving goats into their pen, their feet on the hard sand, their crowding, their velocity and strength.

I was crying.

I wanted to leave my body behind.

I had been deceived. Everything promised had turned into illusion, rotten, nothing but dust in my hands. They had betrayed me. I had not become beautiful. I didn't radiate. Instead I had fallen into an abyss. And now, upon landing, there to meet me was the cold blue pain that my body never forgot.

There was no comfort. Everyone was busy.

I felt walls growing up, separating me from those I loved.

Months later my joints began to ache. On waking in the morning, I'd bend my legs to stand. But no sooner would I be up than I would feel cramping in both feet. When I'd reach for the washing bowl, a pricking and pounding announced itself inside my wrists. I was always coughing.

"Drink goat's milk," my mother said. She was always up before me. I shook my head. I wasn't hungry. "Drink," she said. "Look how thin you are." Instead, I took a sip of water. I had never been a big eater, but now I began giving Adan my leftover corn porridge.

I wasn't eating because I couldn't.

Anyway, why should I? It was enough to drink a little water mornings and evenings. I took my staff and went out to the goats. Behind the dunes the sun had begun to show: white, clear, pure.

What would happen, I suddenly thought, if my parents died?

What if I died? Who would weep at my grave? Would my mother throw herself in the dust? Would my father wail? Would my sisters mourn for their lost sister? I pushed the thoughts aside. I didn't understand where they had come from, but stubbornly, they came over and over again.

I drove the goats to an isolated clearing. My toes were

deformed, and my knees and ankles continued to swell to the size of ripe grapefruits. The other girls laughed at me and called me names. They taunted me, saying that I'd never find a husband, that no one would marry a cripple. And I could no longer run after them to beat them up. When they climbed trees, jumped over rocks, or stood on their hands, I stood apart.

Although it was hot, I wasn't thirsty. But the goats were. They were constantly pulling on each other's teats. I drove them toward a clearing of myrrh. Once there, I let the animals be and sat in the shade with my thighs pressed together, not cross-legged. Girls weren't supposed to sit with their thighs pressed together but I wanted to protect myself. Never again would anybody touch me there. Whenever I thought of the excisor's wrinkled face and her bony fingers, I felt an icy pain run up my spine. Every single cell in my body remembered.

With a piece of bark I dug a hole in the sand to cool my swollen ankles. Slowly the sun crawled through its orbit and I waited for the time to pass.

In the evening, while I was milking the herd, Anisa stood at the edge of the pen. She had brought me berries and held them out: thick juice was running through her fingers.

"Go away," I said. "You're dirty."

Anisa looked at me, and in her eyes I recognized an expression that I knew only too well. I, too, would have felt dirty, since for so many years they'd hammered it into me. Now I was clean. But I really didn't feel that way.

Still, I flaunted it.

Just like the other girls.

A year passed, and I still couldn't walk without pain. My toes were twisted bone, my knees were stiff, and often I would totter on the outer sides of my feet. Every evening my ankles were swollen. They looked like balls of dust left lying on the ground that had gotten drenched in rain and enlarged to double and triple their original size.

In the morning my mother fanned embers into flame. Then she extinguished the fire, dug out and wrapped the hot earth in a cloth, and placed the compress on my legs. Warmed like this, I could sometimes move them. "You're getting grandma's illness," my mother said. Grandma's joints had also become deformed, but much later in life. And my cough grew worse. At some point tuberculosis was mentioned. I sat around, unable to make myself useful. No longer a worker, I had become a burden.

Slowly I grew more and more bitter.

One night I dreamed that my family had buried me. My parents and siblings stood in a half circle around my grave. I felt them throw earth on me, every clump thudding through my shroud. I shouted, "I'm not dead! I'm not dead!" But with unmoving faces they stared into the depth at a white cloth, a dead body. My father stayed behind at the gravesite after the others had gone. And then he, too, turned away. Very clearly I heard his footsteps fade.

Screaming, panting for breath, I woke up.

One morning my mother said to my father, "Take her to town, to your brother. He's rich. He should take Fadumo to a doctor. But . . ." and my mother covered her face with both hands before reaching toward the sky in prayer. "But, Allah be praised, bring her back to me!"

Sad but excited I said good-bye to everyone: Jama and Adan and Muhammad, Nadifo and Saïd, Uncle Yusuf, his wives and their children. My mother accompanied us to the fence. There she stopped, and hugged and kissed me. Then my father and I set off.

Every time I turned around, I saw my mother still standing at the fence. Her left hand on her hip, she waved to us. The image burned itself into my memory. The path was hard and dusty, the sun ablaze, and the farther away we got, the smaller the gesturing form became. Eventually, the red earth swallowed her.

My father marched, his staff twirling in the air, his feet flying over the sand. And all the time, he talked. In the city, he said, I had to watch out. There were streets and cars and a lot of strangers, not all of whom were well-intentioned. I tried to take in all of his advice. I remembered cars but I had to ask myself, what's a street? And, why are people bad? After a while I was out of breath. I decided not to talk anymore and only to walk. Soon I was exhausted.

"Oh dear, child," my father called back to me, as if he'd only just realized that he was six feet, six inches tall, and I half that and sick to boot. He tried to slow his pace but he soon fell into his customary rhythm. For a nomad, a two days' march is a stroll. Even larger distances can be covered with breathtaking speed, since he's focused on a goal. When my father noticed that I had started to cry from exhaustion, he lifted me onto his shoulders and asked what I saw from up there. "A hill," I answered.

"What does it look like?"

"Like a camel seat: gentle and brown."

"What else do you see?"

"An acacia." I shivered. "And an incense bush."

"Do you see dust? Do you see other nomads on their way?"

I turned my head in all directions. "No."

"Do you see smoke? A place where people are living? Where we can get something to drink?"

"No." Each nomad in the desert is obliged to give water to others whenever they ask. I already knew that. Every wanderer will also be asked to eat. It's the custom. But we were alone. "No, Papa, I see only the steppe."

We walked until dark. Then my father spread a mat and lit a fire. I sat in his arms with my head against his chest and his beard tickling my head. For the first time in my life I had him all to myself. For the first time in a long time I no longer felt sad. Somewhere a hyena howled but I knew my father had a dagger; whatever happened, he'd protect me.

"My sunshine," he said and caressed my hair. I asked permission to massage his feet. My father hummed a song by an old Somali poet, but it sounded awful. I just had to laugh and cough. Holding my ears, I begged him to stop. My father was my hero, but singing was one thing he couldn't do.

Later we listened to the cracking of the twigs as they burned. I wanted to hold on to every second, but my eyelids drooped. I fell asleep with my father's aroma of tobacco and coffee still in my nostrils.

In the morning, my father gave me some water and, out of a little sack that he was carrying, took two dried pieces of camel meat. He also gave me a sweet chunk of gelatin made of butter and sugar. I broke a piece off. Chewing, I asked, "What's it like at Uncle Abdulkadir's?"

"You'll see."

"Where does he live, and where will we stay?"

"In Mogadishu."

"What does it look like?"

"It's a big city with a lot of houses and people."

"And what does Uncle Abdulkadir look like?"

"He's a handsome man."

"And why is he so important?"

"Because he owns the largest printing company in Somalia."

"What's a printing company?"

"They make newspapers. And passports."

"What are passports? What are newspapers?"

"You'll see."

My father stood up, took a shallow swallow from the water bottle and tied up our provisions in his little sack. I tried to imagine what newspapers and passports and streets might be like. And my uncle. Supposedly he was a tall man, much larger than my father!

We set off, and when I grew weaker, my father carried me on his shoulders. It was unusual to see a man carrying his eight-year-old daughter on his shoulders, but my joints were as thick as ripened fruit. In the afternoon we met a nomadic family who invited us to eat with them and replenish our water supply. The family manufactured shoes from rubber tires, and my father bought a pair. The sandals had thick soles, impermeable to thorns or stones. And they didn't stink as our leather footwear did. But a glance at me and my father said, "You're growing too quickly. If I bought you a pair of shoes, in no time they'd no longer fit."

Then we left.

On the third day we reached a city.

The houses were stone, like in the village, and reached to the skies. I didn't understand how they could keep their balance and not tip over. Even more confusing were the throngs of people running around like termites: men in uniforms like my oldest brother Ahmed's; girls in uniforms that barely reached their knees made of fabric that caught the sun and glistened; women in multicolored *dirrahs* and, what surprised me, in all different patterns. At home we often all wore the same fabric because when my father bought a bolt of cloth, my mother sewed for the entire family.

All the people were rushing around. Where were they going? Where had they come from?

Voices sounded everywhere. The air was dry and full of dust. I felt hemmed in. Somebody bumped into me and I lost my balance. My joints hurt. A boy zapped by so close that I felt the wind of his flight. A man moved past sitting on a metal contraption with two wheels. Deftly he wove through the crowd. It all looked very odd, and I was surprised that he didn't fall off. A woman dragged a box behind her on which she'd piled red fruit. This box had wheels as well. I became seriously dizzy. Openmouthed I stared at all the activity. Behind me a noise, then a piercing whistle. An animal? Something was coming directly toward me.

A hand shoved me aside.

"In the city you can't simply stand around in the middle of the street," my father warned. I stared down. Under my feet was a bright swathe of compacted sand. That was a street.

"When a car honks, you have to jump aside," my father explained.

With the tinny clang still in my ears, I objected. "But an animal walks around me when I'm in the way."

"A car isn't an animal. A car will run you over."

I looked at my father and after the receding automobile. If a car wasn't an animal, what was it? And why didn't it behave like a camel?

"A car can't see," my father explained. "It can't hear and can't feel."

"But how can it move all by itself?"

"Somebody's driving it."

I was totally confused.

"Come here. You can walk close to the houses."

"But there are too many people."

"Well, that's the city."

My father walked along the roadway, as people moved out of his way and he moved out of theirs. Behind him I followed, bending and stretching, looking around, out of breath, curious, overwhelmed by the newness, the magnificence all more colorful than I had imagined. Still, I missed the breadth and silence of the steppe. Never before had I been surrounded by more people than those in my own family or clan. The hubbub seemed strange. "Stay close to me," my father ordered. "Don't walk away." Sometimes next to each other, often in single file, we proceeded down the street. My feet hurt and my knees were stiff. "We'll eat in a restaurant," my father announced. I remained quiet. I didn't want to ask again what something meant.

We reached a house in which people were sitting not on the floor but on chairs. Some held steaming bowls in their hands; some had placed the bowls on wooden boards. I did as my father did, and sat down on a chair. "Never eat any meat," he warned. "You never know if it's fresh."

I nodded, happy to sit down. A woman brought milk and rice. The rice was brown and swam in a liquid that stank. I preferred to sip the milk. It tasted watery. "You've thinned my milk," I called after the waitress.

"Is that true?" my father gripped the glass. At home, when we milked the sheep, goats, and cows, the milk was frothy, fresh, warm, and delicious. Often you tasted the herbs with which we'd treated the bowls and milk containers. Sometimes the milk was fatty, in which case it helped to still our hunger. From some animals the milk was thinner and quenched our thirst. But what had been offered here tasted like my mother's efforts to stretch the milk with water in times of drought. Angry, my father tasted it and called, "I want my money back."

Later my father and I reached the dwelling of an unfriendly woman who showed us where we could sleep in her courtyard. The ground was cold and hard. As in my aunt's village by the river, there was an outhouse, and this time my father insisted that I learn how to use it. The stench was horrendous. I held my breath, squatted over the hole in the ground and did my business as fast as I could. The woman's small children, who were playing in the yard, were dirty and rude. I chose to have nothing to do with them. I said only that I was on my way to the big city to my famous uncle. "Do you know my uncle?"

Without a word they looked at me and shook their heads.

The truck was gigantic and full of people who shoved and pushed. Each was trying to squeeze past the person ahead. Women and children were hoisted up as there was no ladder and nothing to hold on to. Sacks of wheat were everywhere. Between the bundles lay goats and sheep with their feet bound. A man ran up and down beside the truck with a list in his hand, calling out names and counting. Everyone was too busy trying to find a spot to respond to him. The sun was high, and I was sweating. The driver shouted something that I couldn't understand and honked the horn loudly. Then he turned on the motor, and a cloud of black smoke enveloped us. It smelled strange—like a promise. The truck bucked and trembled and then began to move. I grabbed the railing and held on tight but slid into a fat woman who smiled, then pushed me away.

Without warning, the driver slammed on the brakes and all the children and goats and wheat sacks and women and men flew into one another. "Everyone out!" the driver ordered.

"Why?" called a man, and then another complained. A group of women scolded, but the driver sharply insisted that everyone get down and that the freight be removed as well. He barked a few orders. Then the men began to haul the sacks back on board, this time taking care to balance the load. My father pulled at his beard and chewed roasted coffee beans. He said: "It's going to shake. You'll have to hold on tight to me, especially when you get tired, or else you'll fall out when you're asleep." Then he gave me a tin can that an old woman had discarded. He smoothed the edges and said, "If you have to spit, use this." I hugged the can and watched the men heaving the sacks from one side to the other. A woman squatted in the sand holding a chicken in her hand. From time to time its wings brushed against me in a hopeless attempt to fly. The woman hit the bird on the head every time it tried. "The best thing would be for you to sit directly behind the driver's cabin," my father whispered. I nodded.

When the driver gave the word, everyone stormed the loading deck. My father lifted me up, and I climbed over the side, ran around the sacks, and squatted behind the metal wall. With hands and feet I defended our chosen spot until my father got there. Most of the passengers were men, since few women went to town. One woman held her sick child immobile in her arms. The men chewed tobacco. The driver hit the horn and finally, after all the women, men, children, goats, sheep, and sacks had been properly arranged, he started the motor, and the town disappeared behind us in a column of smoke and dust.

For four days we drove on poorly marked tracks, on pitted roads and rutted trails. When the driver stopped for the first time, a woman lifted me down from the platform. In the sand, crouching behind a thorn bush, I felt my body continue to twitch in the rhythm of the pockmarked roadway. The air was hot and dusty and coughs scratched at my throat. Sand and flies attacked me, biting my skin. The men chatted, chewed tobacco, and spit. Sometimes the wind, coming from the wrong direction, landed a wad on my arm or leg or cheek. The sick child cried, and the woman had to hold it over the railing when it threw up. Every time we approached a clump of trees, the driver leaned out of the cabin and shouted "Watch out!" Everybody drew in their heads. Then the branches flew over us, though not before a twig tore one man's ear off. The truck pounded on over ruts as big as waterholes, bounced people high out of their improvised seats, settled them with groans, threw them to one side, and rolled them back and forth.

From the truck floor I peered out at a landscape that stretched to the horizon. From time to time we passed a village. Sometimes the houses were made of stone, sometimes of clay. I saw leather roofs stretched over walls. Shrubbery glowed a strange carmine in the sun. As we passed very close by, I could see that red dust powdered the leaves. Occasionally another truck appeared, and, with a good deal of commotion, the drivers tried to maneuver their vehicles past one another without forcing one of them to leave the track worn in the sand and risk breaking an axel. I saw nomads holding their camels back so that they would not bolt from fright, and I waved and shouted, asking the nomads whether they had seen my family, did they know where they were. My father looked at me. "How small the world is," he laughed.

The dust crept into every bodily opening and itched. The driver stopped only rarely because he was chewing khat, leaves from a plant whose juice gave him energy. Whenever he did stop, we got down and bought tea. My father complained because the tea was insubstantial and the sellers were stingy with the sugar. When we stopped at a wooden building to get gas, I leaned over the railing and saw a thick hose placed in a hole on the side of the truck. The attendant was not very skillful since he kept spilling the gas. I took a deep breath. I actually liked the strange, slightly spicy aroma.

With the motor running, you could hear a deep drumming, a rustling and knocking, a noise like beating on a tom tom. I heard the rhythm and felt the vibration all over my body. We drove through cities with asphalt roads and odors of their own: precious, herbal. Too excited, I couldn't eat, and, like everybody else, all the bones in my body hurt. Eventually I spied dunes on the horizon, and, overcome with fatigue, I fell asleep.

In the evenings the driver would stop in a village. Everyone would help to unload the animals, feed them, and give them water, and the passengers would spread mats on the sand. It was not as clean as on the steppe. Two men guarded the load while the water supply was refreshed. The goats were tied to posts for the night. I felt sorry for them because with their bound feet they could hardly move. Some of them wounded themselves by rubbing their limbs together, and they bleated in complaint. Nomads, I thought, would never treat their animals that way.

Soldiers stood at a tollgate. They wore uniforms, carried rifles, and commanded us to get out on the double. The driver grumbled about being treated like a criminal, and the soldiers told him roughly to hold his tongue. With their rifles in hand some inspected the cabin, while others climbed onto the back. My father warned me to be quiet. Everyone was glad once we got on with the journey.

Finally we arrived in Somalia's capital, Mogadishu.

The asphalt led there straight as an arrow. To the left and the right stood houses surrounded by lawns, and trees were everywhere. Vines, some with colorful flowers, climbed the walls of houses. The bright green blinded me. Houses were painted yellow and blue; everywhere, color dominated. I saw cars and people, and not a single animal. I saw wooden poles that held ropes fastened to the walls of houses, and I wondered what they were for. Did people hang out their laundry or dry their meat on those lines?

I besieged my father with questions, wanting to understand everything.

He just shook his head and answered, "I don't know, child, where all these people come from, where they're going, what they're called, or who their families are. I couldn't know it all." I didn't understand. Till now my father had always known everything!

The truck turned the corner into an even more crowded part of the city. Here the cars drove next to each other, honking and butting like nervous goats. There were large cars and small ones, and I wondered whether the little cars were the children of the big ones. In the middle of the throng a donkey cart lumbered along, and for a moment I felt sorry for the donkey immersed in so many cars and so much noise.

Then something simply took my breath away. At the end of the street stood a man, larger than I had ever seen, gigantic, towering over everyone. He was dressed entirely in black, including the cloth slung around his hips. Stiffly the man stared down at the roadway, the people, the cars, the donkey.

"What's that, Papa?" I whispered.

"A statue."

"What's a statue? And what's the man doing? Look. He's holding something in his hand. A stone? Is he going to throw it?"

"He's not alive. People built him out of stone."

I looked from my father, to the statue, and back again to my father. For a moment I doubted his word. But now the truck drove directly toward the stone man! I was afraid. He kept growing bigger. Now he towered over my head, and his shadow had already fallen on me. What would happen if he toppled over?

Why had they made him so indescribably large?

Why would anyone build stone people?

I closed my eyes.

When I opened them again, the man had disappeared, but I had no time to think about him. Honking, the truck turned a corner and squealed as the driver hit the brakes. With a stammer and cough the motor died. The driver shouted something that I didn't understand, and everyone stood up, including my father. "We're here, child." His red hair glowed in the sun. He looked tired.

Behind me, men were pushing, women calling, goats complaining and nudging me with their horns. Someone started to unload the sacks. One man shouted and then another. They were fighting over the sacks—they all looked the same to me. Nobody knew which ones belonged to whom anymore. When one sack fell to the ground and split open, small boys suddenly appeared—where had they come from so quickly? With naked hands and with bowls, they scooped up the grain, filling their pockets and kerchiefs. Men shouted at the boys and struck them. Many of the boys ran away; a few begged. The goats bleated; cars sped by. The driver yelled, making a strange sound, his lips full of khat. Green juice ran out of the corner of his mouth. The sick baby cried. My father pulled me along behind him until we turned into a side street. Here it was quieter, although people still bumped into us, their elbows hitting my head, their legs rubbing against mine. Nobody seemed to watch where they were going. No one seemed considerate.

"Watch out, you dirty country girl!" a woman yelled.

I stared at her. Why was she so unfriendly to me?

My father strode on in silence, dragging me into an alley. My legs had begun to ache. "Stay right here and wait for me," he said, and lifted me up onto a container in front of a house. On the other side of the street a few people were sitting, some with animals beside them, others with sacks and baskets of fruit. "Don't move, no matter what happens. I'll be right back." Before I could respond, he disappeared into the crowd.

The wall of the house felt cool when I leaned back against it. Flies landed on my legs and crawled over my arms and face. Strong odors from across the street reached me, and the humid air felt heavy. I stared at the women wearing beautiful cloth, not wraparounds but white gowns of thin fabric that they seemed to have thrown over themselves without having to tie, lace, or knot anything. The fabric reached to the ground. Such clothing would have been very impractical for a nomad: How could you run after the goats dressed that way? My stomach began to rumble. I couldn't remember when I had last eaten. Carefully I slid off the container and crossed the street. Looking around, I was aware that, were my father to come back right then, I'd be able to see him. I wove past people on their mats. On a board lay silver animals, small and very flat, some still twitching. "What are those?" I asked a boy squatting next to the board and sharpening a stick.

"Fish," he answered. "You're pretty dumb."

"I'm not dumb. And your fish—they stink!" I went farther. A

short distance away red fruit lay on the sand. They were round with smooth skin and looked delicious. I took one, stroked it, and sniffed. "Hey," screamed a woman. "Put that tomato down at once!" Shocked, I let the fruit fall. "You couldn't possibly have any money, judging by the way you look!" Her voice was shrill, like a goat during a hard birth. "Money?" she shouted as if I were deaf, and bent down, a wicked grin on her face. She was sweating. I could see the beads on the bridge of her nose. In her hand was a rod. I got out of there fast.

Never before had anyone stopped me from eating a piece of fruit!

I returned to the container. My father was nowhere in sight. I sat down, straightened the scarf to protect my head from the sun, and waited. And sweated. But I didn't dare move away again.

Time passed.

At some point the sun reached the middle of the sky. The people across the street took their animals and fruit and rolled up their mats. They left behind an empty space with the stench of dead fish. Nowhere was there a speck of shade! I was thirsty, and coughs wracked my throat. I started to worry. What could have happened to my father? Had he gotten lost? How could I find my uncle all alone? A group of boys sauntered down the road and stopped to scrounge inside a container at the side of the square. Then they spotted me. Their leader bent down and picked something up. He was much bigger than I, and even from a distance I could see that his teeth were entirely brown. He pulled his arm back and threw the stone at me. He hit only the container. It rocked. Another boy threw the next stone—then another and another. "Country girl!" they shouted. "Nomad!"

"You dirty nomad girl!" the leader shouted and picked up an even bigger stone. I ducked but didn't dare to run away. The stones hit my arms and my feet. Just then, a black and yellow car sped into the alley. There was a screeching of breaks, the car doors burst open, and my father flew out and threw his arms around me. Before I could open my mouth, he'd lifted me off the container, run back to the car, and placed me onto the backseat. The driver quickly sped away.

Houses and people flew past us in a single stream. The car moved more quickly than I could run, more quickly than I had ever raced in my life. My father said something to the driver, who laughed, honked, and waved his arms. My father wasn't afraid. I bit my lips. Stiff and straight as a tree trunk, I sat on the backseat. That was my first ride in a taxi.

Smiling, my father turned around and looked at me. "I'm really very forgetful," he joked and his beard shook with cheerfulness. He told me how he had bought gifts for the relatives, had gotten into the taxi and driven to my uncle's house at the other end of the city. On getting out he had said, "Let's go child," only to remember, in response to the driver's strange look, that he had left his daughter in the chaos of the town.

In Mogadishu

3

He had the same wonderful feet as my father: large but with fine bones, long toes, bright nails, and a powerful heel. They appeared in sandals with leather straps that adorned the top of his foot. A silver buckle shone on his ankle. His soles looked as soft as dune sand. His feet passed, almost silent.

Their owner didn't see me.

The watchman went ahead and drove the car into the shade. My uncle disappeared. A door closed, and stillness filled the garden. I felt I had seen a vision. Only the perfume that lingered in the air told me that he'd passed by.

Since early morning I'd been sitting in the garden in the shade of a tree, surrounded by grasses and sweet-smelling flowers that glowed yellow and orange and pink, so strong and plump that I wanted to taste them. When the watchman wasn't looking, I ran my tongue over the cool leaves and tasted their sweetness. A bush, as tall as a man and filled with little glowing blossoms as blue as the sky, the color of my scarf, drew me to it. Curious, I stroked its leaves. I would have loved to pluck a flower to show my mother. The watchman said that my uncle had gone to work and would be back in the afternoon and that my father had asked him to look after me while he visited relatives. At some point the watchman asked me, "Do you want to read the paper?"

I nodded, not wanting to embarrass myself.

The newspaper's large sheets of paper crackled and swished when moved. On all sides I saw nothing but signs. I looked for the letters that the Qur'anic school teacher had put on his slate, but I couldn't recognize any. Between the letters were pictures of people. When I saw the first one, I drew back in fear. For a moment, I thought the man in the paper might move, might talk to me. I remembered the horribly big statue. And my father's radio—a holy object that he took on his travels and guarded when he was at home. I had turned the little box on its head, turned the dials, shaken it, and looked for the little people who were talking and singing. They must have been very small, I thought. How else could they have fit inside? But who fed them? I had pressed the radio to my mouth and shouted, "Are you hungry?" My sister Khadija had laughed at me and said I was stupid because there weren't any people in there. But she was also unable to say where the voices came from.

"That's our president," a voice said. It was the watchman, whom I had forgotten. "Surely you know our president?" I took the precaution of nodding. His finger pointed to a photograph. The man in the picture was wearing a cap and carried a rifle but he was small, a lot smaller than I, so he was not very impressive.

"And that's the Somali national flag."

Again, I nodded.

"Here's a pencil. You can draw a little." The watchman tugged at his belt and wiped his forehead with his hand. He smiled. I took the pencil.

I began to copy the letters from the newspaper, following their lines, curves, and dots. I took pains not to slip up with the pencil or make ugly marks but tried to write neatly like a schoolgirl. But the pencil lay like a stranger in my fist. The joints of my fingers had long been too stiff to fold themselves around the shaft. I was so busy concentrating that I looked up only when I became conscious of a sound that was beginning to become familiar. A car had entered the driveway. Behind the wheel was my uncle. He wore a bright white shirt, and his hair was damp. Slowly he rolled past with the window half down. He glanced at me and at the newspaper. Again I smelled his perfume. I saw his beard, his soft lips, and his gray hair, and I nearly laughed. My father had told me his brother was younger—how could he have gray hair? The watchman ran to open the gate. My uncle drove off. Obviously he didn't know who I was. He probably thought I was a beggar, somebody whom others should take care of.

Later in the afternoon the car returned. The watchman opened the gate. I looked up from my newspaper. My handsome uncle strode across the lawn, suit jacket over one arm, one hand in his pocket. He looked more elegant than any person I had ever seen. Immediately the watchman began to clean the car, spraying it with water and rubbing it. His energy reminded me of my father and other men caring for camels. Suddenly my uncle looked in my direction. He hesitated. Then he came toward me, where I could admire his beautiful feet again. He bent his head and asked, "Who are you?"

I whizzed through my family tree. "I'm Fadumo Abdi Hersi Farah Husen." The rage that had accumulated little by little throughout the day exploded then. "And who are you," I asked, "that you don't even know the names of your brother's children?" I was too hurt to be well-behaved and respectful. My uncle chuckled, amused. His gray beard covered his chin and crept up to the ears on either side like a frame around his face, leaving his cheeks free.

My uncle pointed to the newspaper. "What are you doing there?"

"You can see what I'm doing. I'm reading!" Uncle Abdulkadir grabbed the newspaper and looked at the letters I'd drawn. His smile grew larger and, finally, he burst into laughter. His sideburns looked blue in the sun. I had not left a single letter out. He ran his hand through his hair and asked, "Would you like to go to school?"

On July 1, 1960, my country was founded. Before that, the colonial powers Italy, England, and France had divided up the Horn of

Africa. Nine years later in 1969, a military coup d'état brought the government down, and a new president, General Siad Barre, another of my uncles, proclaimed the Socialist Republic of Somalia.

With Soviet support, the country followed the socialist model: Political parties were forbidden and political education was introduced. Somalia established compulsory elementary education, standardized script, literacy courses, development campaigns, and equality for women. The new regime said it opposed the strong clan system and cronyism. Siad Barre, however, placed his family into important posts.

Uncle Abdulkadir, a half brother of my father, had been brought to Mogadishu as a child and sent to school. Later he studied agriculture in the Netherlands. In 1969, when Uncle Abdulkadir returned to Somalia, President Siad Barre turned the government printing office over to him and, with it, the control of newspapers, passports, school texts, and propaganda. Uncle Abdulkadir enlarged the state apparatus, sent staff to the German Democratic Republic for training, bought modern machinery in Germany, and traveled to Europe often.

Uncle Abdulkadir was not a politician. He was a family man, and he accepted the challenge the president had offered.

Five people lived with my uncle in his house: his wife, Madeleine, their daughter Idil and son Qamaan, as well as two informally adopted children, Saïda and my cousin Ahmed, whose father had been killed in a clan war between Hawiyes and Marehans. Each room was larger than the hut that had housed my entire family in the steppe.

Uncle Abdulkadir brought me to my cousins' room. Two large windows revealed a garden, but surrounding walls hid the horizon. "Why do you live so closed in?" I asked. Uncle Abdulkadir laughed. So did Saïda and Idil, but their laughter sounded less friendly. Under the ceiling a fan whirled. "What's that?" I asked.

"A ventilator."

"Who's moving it?"

"No one. Electric current moves it."

The answer made no sense to me.

The ground floor held a built-in kitchen. "I ordered it from Quelle's catalogue," Uncle Abdulkadir explained, "in Germany." I didn't understand a thing, but my uncle seemed to be very proud of the kitchen. "Look," he said. "A stove. And a sink. And . . ." He stepped aside so I could get a better look. "A refrigerator!" Uncle Abdulkadir opened the door. An icy breath stroked my arms, and suddenly it became colder in the kitchen than at night on the steppes. "Are you thirsty?" he asked. I nodded. He filled a glass and handed it to me. I took a sip but I thought my mouth would explode! I spit the liquid out on the floor and screamed, "Are you trying to kill me?" My cousins—the boys and the girls—doubled over with laughter. Uncle Abdulkadir tried to calm me down. "It was only water," he explained, "with ice cubes."

"That's not water," I complained.

I was confused. Overwhelmed. Impressed.

In the bathroom, water fell from the ceiling like rain from the sky, and they told me I ought to step under it to wash. The toilet looked like a stool with a hole in the middle. I feared falling in, or that a hand might emerge to grab me. They showed me a cord to pull. When I did, the force of the water filling the bowl sprayed me and the wall behind me. I jumped aside in fright. In the middle of the room was a coffin that was made of metal instead of wood. You could sit in it and bathe. Everywhere water bubbled—clean, clear, cool water. It was never brown with lumps of earth or clay in it. It was never tasteless or overheated by the sun. I drank it until my stomach crackled. I used both hands, slurped, spit, and kept on drinking it just for fun, even though I'd long since quenched my thirst. Water on my lips, I nibbled, licked, and let it run over my tongue.

It felt as though I had landed in another universe.

I was awed by the life of city people, and my astonishment never ceased. I learned that when you pushed a button, a light appeared. In the middle of the darkest night, city folks could see. They were fully independent of the sun. They had sand-soft feet, and the skin on their hands was as tender as cat fur; thorns and barbed bushes had never touched them. The women washed their hair daily and combed it, decorated their faces with colorful pencils, and sprayed themselves with sweet-smelling waters. They ate thin, meter-long noodles with a red sauce, using metal tools. When I was alone with my cousins, they pulled at my robe, giggled, and talked about foreign countries and math. "You can't even add," Saïda, the older one, teased.

"I can subtract five from seven," I answered and didn't understand why they burst out laughing.

A physician gave me medicine for my cough and, several times a day, the nanny brought me a plate of sliced mangoes and papayas.

The chauffeur drove me to a tailor. She was a heavy old woman who, for several minutes, looked me up and down, scowling. Suddenly she expelled air through her front teeth. "The child is skin and bone," she hissed. Sighing, she grabbed a tape measure and pulled on my wraparound. I was afraid she wanted to take it away so I held on tight. "You can't go to school in that," the stranger snapped. "You need a uniform." With the tape she measured my arms and legs.

When the skirt and blouse arrived, I was shocked. The skirt reached only to my knees! "I can't go out on the street looking like that!" I whined. "I'm a lady. I'm almost old enough to get married. I need a long skirt." So Uncle Abdulkadir had it lengthened a few centimeters. Thus outfitted, I was sent to school. I was so delighted not to be looking after goats from morning to evening that, before you could turn around, I learned all the Arabic and Latin letters, as well as numbers.

Everyone was astonished.

Three months later when the school holidays began, my uncle sent me to the hospital. The doctors diagnosed me as underweight, but I did not have tuberculosis. They prescribed vitamins and instructed me to eat more so that, with Allah's help, I'd become a good and even pretty young lady. Several times a day nurses' helpers would come to give me injections. Nearly all the children cried when they got shots, but I was brave, clenched my teeth, and won praise. I became friendly with a few nurses who took me with them on their rounds and allowed me to distribute medicines. They taught me how to give injections; soon I was giving myself my own shots and bragging to the other children. After six weeks I was released, a couple of kilos heavier and nearly free of pain. In the meantime my father had left the city to return to the steppe, which made me very sad. I couldn't wait to show my mother what I'd learned in school. But Uncle Abdulkadir had decided that, for the time being anyway, I'd be staying in Mogadishu.

In Somali families, it's customary for these wealthier members to take care of their poorer siblings' children.

Aunt Madeleine took me under her wing.

She was small and dynamic with light, Arabic-looking skin. No matter the time of day, she was perfectly coiffed. Like my uncle, she went regularly for a manicure. Both of them used wonderful perfumes. Elegant as she was, I was not surprised that Aunt Madeleine spoke several languages. But when she spoke to us children in Somali, she made odd mistakes. She would confuse personal pronouns, for instance, and say: "He doesn't like it" instead of "I don't like it."

Confused, I'd look around me and ask, "Who, Aunt? Who doesn't like it?" until she noticed her mistake.

Aunt Madeleine placed great importance on raising and educating children, especially girls. She'd say, "Women have to show they're stronger than men," and "What you have in your head, no one can take away from you." On the evening when I first met her, she wore a green suit, her hair beautifully arranged, her lips and fingernails a blazing red. She danced through the house on high heels, almost as if she were floating, reminding me of stories about man-eaters who hovered over graveyards at midnight. Their nails were blood red too.

But I quickly fell in love with Aunt Madeleine.

She taught me how to behave. She told me to use a handkerchief instead of picking my nose, and to use the spittoon in the bathroom—if I had to spit—instead of spitting on the floor. She taught me to eat with a fork and knife. Every evening the family gathered in the salon around a large table that the servants had set with decorative napkins. Uncle Abdulkadir straightened Aunt Madeleine's chair and escorted her to her seat. She unfolded her napkin, spread it on her lap, and placed her hands on the table. "Face toward the plate," she warned, "but not over the plate." I sat up straight. The servants served.

Aunt Madeleine reached for her silverware, lightly speared her meat, cut a small piece off, and placed it in her mouth. I followed her lead. But my movements were awkward. The knife squeaked, the sauce splattered, and sometimes the vegetables fled the plate, or a piece of meat sailed across the table. The soup ran down my arm, making puddles at my elbow. In the steppe we held pieces of meat with our teeth while cutting off pieces small enough to swallow. I was actually very good at that; not once had I sliced open my lips.

"Small portions," my aunt warned. "It's not nice to stuff your mouth. And sit up straight, child." Her tone was strict, but she never slapped me—neither my aunt nor my uncle ever struck the children. Though I tried hard to do what Aunt Madeline attempted to teach me, I was sometimes so busy thinking about the instructions—the succession of small steps to be managed in a certain order at a certain pace and with a certain agility—that I seldom had any appetite when my uncle called us to the table. I was especially not hungry on days when spaghetti was served.

Aunt Madeleine advised me to keep my head up, to lift my feet, never to slump, and to refrain from scratching my neck. She made me practice a graceful walk with a pile of books on my head. She made sure I was properly dressed and bought me clothes— exquisitely beautiful things—that all belonged to me alone. Previously I had owned little more than a wraparound! She bought leather shoes for me, along with white socks and underpants, although it wasn't clear to me what purpose they served. "A lady never goes without," was Aunt Madeleine's only reply.

Soon I began to imitate my aunt. I tried to move as she did. Like her, I sorted my clothes by color. I was in awe of her authority and tried to use a similarly confident tone when speaking to the servants. "You're a brown noser," my cousins taunted. "You're sucking up to her." That was true. I wanted Aunt Madeleine and Uncle Abdulkadir to be proud of me, to accept me as a daughter.

When the new school year began, my uncle sent me to a private academy taught by English and Italian nuns. Classes started at 7 a.m. We assembled in the courtyard, a sister hoisted the flag, and we all sang in praise of our country: The earth is our mother; the sky, our father; the flag, our protector. Finished, we saluted and went to class.

I worked very hard. Still I found it luxurious to spend the entire day in a shaded room, sitting, thinking, and learning. I did want my cousin Saïda to stop harassing me. She had been at school for three years and she was more clever than I. That made me angry. But it was mainly the school that made me aware that I was different from the other children. Writing and drawing required my best efforts, and at recess I couldn't run around. I avoided any unnecessary movement to spare my joints. As long as they weren't swollen, no one noticed that I was ill. I hid my hands and avoided open-toed sandals. Because I succeeded in hiding my condition, the nuns thought I was merely lazy and not trying hard enough to write neatly. As punishment, I was beaten. So I tried even harder to do math and draw and write until my handwriting was almost as tidy as the others'. I hid my handicap cleverly.

Until my illness attracted no more attention.

Banana fields and mango plantations, coconut palms and acres of grapefruit trees sped past, one after the other. The sun blazed but the breeze cooled the air to a comfortable temperature. I stretched my arm out the window, my fingers tapping in time to the music as we rolled along the country road. It was Friday—the Islamic holiday. Like all wealthy families in the capital we had spent the afternoon at the beach and were now heading for a restaurant. I loved these expeditions in the car. Uncle Abdulkadir was the first person in Somalia to own the 1972 Audi 80 and I loved listening to the music, flaunting my clothes, and showing off a little.

The restaurant Uncle Abdulkadir had chosen sat on the edge of a plantation. The branches of an unusually inviting acacia had been pulled down to make a kind of bower, and for a second I was reminded of the tree under which I had been infibulated. But here the earth was strewn with mats woven in a traditional pattern so beautiful that you weren't supposed to walk on them with shoes. Guests sat on the floor, in front of gigantic plates of delicious dishes the cook had prepared on an open fire. We ate with our fingers. "It's important," Uncle Abdulkadir said, "that you should move easily in both worlds, the modern and the traditional."

Three waiters in white aprons carried trays and served goat steaks, curried rice, and roasted onions with a sauce made of red and green chili, coriander, tomatoes, and garlic. To go with it was *mufo*, cornmeal rolls shaped like cigars. Small bowls contained warm lemon water for cleaning one's fingers. Uncle Abdulkadir offered the spirits a forkful of rice and then we began to eat. My boy cousin, Qamaan, sat silently observing, as he almost always did. Saïda, Idil, and Ahmed ate nicely. But I won, no contest. Although I had become as skilled in eating with a knife and fork as my cousins, they did not have my skill of eating by hand. The restaurant was full, and Uncle Abdulkadir and Aunt Madeleine were constantly greeted by friends. Both were welcome guests at parties and receptions in town. In that respect, my uncle was quite different from other Somali men, who didn't socialize easily.

Sometimes Uncle Abdulkadir put on an apron and cooked. My cousins and I giggled when we spied him at the stove. At first we actually refused to eat what he had prepared. A meal cooked by a man couldn't possibly taste good! But it was wonderful! If we behaved, Uncle Abdulkadir would show us photographs from his student years in Holland. In the pictures he was wearing a thick coat and looked like a king. He had gone ice-skating and he told us that, during winters in Holland, lakes froze along with streets and sidewalks—the entire country, in fact—so that you were constantly falling on your face since it was so slippery. In Mogadishu that was something we, with 40 degrees Celsius—104 degrees Fahrenheit—in the shade, could hardly imagine. He told us about the prejudice that he and other black students encountered, the rejections they had endured.

The waiters served tea with cardamom, cinnamon, and cloves, and with it, milk and cake. Aunt Madeleine snapped open her case and pulled out a long, white cigarette, which Uncle Abdulkadir lit. He encouraged me to form my own opinion about everything and to reject subordination. "I want you to think," he said. "Women have to go through life with their heads held high." He forbade me to serve him. After years of having been raised by my parents to serve with absolute humility and obedience, this was a challenging directive. But I learned to adapt.

Adaptability is a nomad's most valuable asset.

With the elegance of any diva, my aunt drew on her cigarette, her fingernails blazing like forbidden fruit. "We're a special family," she said. My aunt had begun to prepare the children for our later lives. Nonetheless, like her husband, it was important to her that we should know how to live independently. "You can become a professor," she said, "but you still have to know how to iron your blouse." My cousins and I hated these pronouncements, but my aunt insisted that we learn to darn, wash clothes, and clean a room.

"But we have servants," Saïda complained.

"You never know if that's going to continue," Aunt Madeleine replied and instructed the cook to give us lessons. He gave me a pan, oil, and a pound of onions. I was supposed to heat the oil and cube the onions—a challenging task that took forever. When I finally threw the chunks into the pan, the oil was so hot that a flame shot up, scorching my hair, eyelashes, and eyebrows, and covering my body with singed spots. The kitchen was a mess and it took days to clean it up. Still, Aunt Madeleine insisted we learn to cook. When Saïda and I served spaghetti with tomato sauce for the first time, Aunt Madeleine and Uncle Abdulkadir, after only a little hesitation, cleaned their plates. No matter what we girls undertook, my uncle never discouraged us.

When we left the restaurant, the sky was dark, and the air was soft. Under a streetlight we got back into our Audi and drove home. I looked at the stars and hummed a tune from an Indian film. For a moment I was queasy with the fear that I might someday lose this privileged life. "Be quiet," my cousin hissed.

Soon afterward the family moved to a new house on the shore of a lake in the middle of a park. The floors were marble and from the terrace you could look out onto the beach. Until recently the Soviet ambassador had lived there. Then, at Uncle Abdulkadir's request and with the president's support, the house was cleared out. It was, after all, government property.

Slowly I began to understand the kind of power my family enjoyed.

When my uncle Siad Barre had announced the founding of the Socialist Republic of Somalia, a new epoch had begun. The country had been independent only for a short time. The new reforms introduced a unified script so that Somalis could read newspapers in their own language instead of being dependent on the English, Italian, or Arabic press. Women were permitted to study: They could become doctors, lawyers, judges, and ministers. It was a euphoric moment—a collective liberation.

Imams and conservatives had protested. The sky would fall on our heads, they prophesized; the land would burn. On the very day that equality of the sexes was declared, two planes collided over a poor quarter of Mogadishu. Hundreds of people died. Despite this apparent sign, progress could not be stopped. Women enrolled in the university. They worked as flight attendants and radio announcers. Skirts got shorter, and some women even wore pants.

Aunt Madeleine came from the only well-known Christian family in Somalia. Her father was a diplomat. She had been raised in England, sent to boarding school, and had completed her education as a foreign-language secretary. Aunt Madeleine was a modern woman. The first woman to drive a car in Mogadishu, she personified progress and was an inspiration for many other Somali women, who began to dye their hair, wear pumps, and get driver's licenses.

Uncle Abdulkadir advised his secretary to shorten her traditional robe to above the ankles so that she did not have to hold it up and had her hands free for work. He saved our servant girl from a forced marriage by buying her freedom through paying her bride price. From his trips to Germany he always brought back the latest Quelle catalogues so that my cousins and I could order skirts and shorts. European industrialists and diplomats from all over the globe visited. The atmosphere was liberal—open to the world. Aunt Madeleine, who owned several hundred pairs of shoes, opened her garden once a month to poor people who came to eat vitamin-rich foods.

My family was respected, wealthy, and influential.

We were in the government. And the government was the family.

The Italian ambassador swayed only a little, but we noticed. His usually military gestures had softened somewhat. The signora talked without letting her husband out of her sight. Her face revealed no emotion: The slightly hardened pull at the corner of her mouth would be visible only to those who knew her well. A few steps away, the French ambassador's wife was chatting with the French chief of protocol. She was wearing an elegant dress of royal blue silk and shoes of the same fabric. A number of German industrialists had told funny stories at dinner. At that point in the evening, the Italian ambassador was almost drunk. The Signora, who knew it, laughed. "I bet he falls into the flowerbed," Saïda joked.

"Shh." I didn't want Aunt Madeleine to hear us. Idil let the curtain fall and imitated the ambassador, caricaturing his movements, staggering across the salon, rolling her eyes. Saïda giggled. "Did you see the wife of the English school director?" she whispered.

"Madame was so hoity-toity, she ate her peas one by one." I burst out laughing but quickly clapped both hands in front of my mouth. For days we had begged Aunt Madeleine to allow us to serve at the reception. When she finally agreed, she taught us to serve from the right, clear things away from the left, how to pour hot gravies, and to balance four plates on one hand. Finally, we began to look professional. Having been allowed to cater at other parties, we were used to adults paying no attention to us, and we hardly noticed them. But at this event we were excited. We studied the guests' gestures and their clothing. When someone was really dressed up, we were amused. When the grown-ups danced, we were embarrassed. They looked so silly—the way they jerked to the rhythm of the music. From time to time they brought their sons and daughters along. Then we'd all run down to the beach house and try to understand English or Italian. Some of the foreign children spoke a little Somali.

"You did very well." Aunt Madeleine entered the salon, heading toward the buffet where she kept her cigarettes. "Everyone was really impressed. My friends said they envy me my well-behaved girls." Her thin eyebrows danced as she laughed. From a drawer she extracted a box.

"Will we be paid?" Saïda asked. Aunt Madeleine hesitated, deliberately taking her time lighting up before pleating her brow.

I laughed. "Please, Aunt, please," I cajoled.

She inhaled and puffed into the air. "A dress?" she asked.

"Bell-bottoms!" Idil cried.

"High heels!" Saïda shouted.

"Uncle Abdulkadir complains when he sees you in such shoes. 'They'll ruin their feet,' he says. And he's right."

"But Mama, they're cool!"

"They're uncomfortable," answered Aunt Madeleine.

"Everybody's wearing them," Saïda begged. Which wasn't true. Only the daughters of rich parents wore jeans and American T-shirts and Italian high heels. Everybody else had to make do with pants, skirts, and blouses made in Somalia or India. Saïda and I had laid our freshly washed jeans out on the sidewalk, weighed them down with stones in a few places, and left them for two days in the sun. After that they were bleached with dark and light blue patches. "You could just buy rags to start with," Aunt Madeleine had shouted, horrified, as we proudly squeezed ourselves into the jeans, now so narrow that you had to lie down to zip them up. She sighed. My glance fell on her red pumps. "I'll tell Uncle Abdulkadir, 'If I buy any other kind of shoes, the girls won't wear them.'"

"Right," Saïda agreed.

"Wouldn't you like to go to the movies? Or buy some new records? Or give a party yourselves?" Aunt Madeleine put out her cigarette in the ashtray. The lipstick on the filter was the exact same color as her nails. "I'll think about it," I said. We hugged her. She grabbed her cigarette case. The heels of her shoes clicked on the marble floor to the rhythm of her graceful steps. At the threshold she stopped and turned. "Saïda, where's that new T-shirt that Uncle Abdulkadir brought you from Paris?"

"I don't know. I wanted to put it on but couldn't find it."

"I'll ask the servants."

"Maybe a thief took it off the line." Aunt Madeleine looked at Saïda. Idil and I looked on innocently. "Took it off the line? Over a wall five yards high?" Now Aunt Madeleine crinkled her brow in earnest. "I can hardly believe that. I think we'd better talk about it in the morning." Then she returned to her guests on the terrace.

Saïda looked unhappy. She had traded the T-shirt for two comic books, Italian original editions of dramatic love stories with taboo kissing scenes that we examined in secret in the garden. My cousin had had to sacrifice one of her better T-shirts to get them.

Sometimes I thought about the steppe, the land without borders, which held nothing but endless space to draw one's gaze. I longed for it then—to stride with broad, free steps. The city confined us, and girls were forbidden to walk in the streets. Instead, a chauffeur drove us everywhere. From time to time I envied other children who went to school on foot.

And I missed my mother.

I loved Aunt Madeleine and Uncle Abdulkadir, but in the evening, before falling asleep, when I thought about the day's events, I might suddenly smell a mixture of herbs and earth, reminding me of the aroma of my mother. I wanted to see my sisters and brothers and my father, too, but the craving was not as painful as the desire to see my mother. This was odd because she had always been the stricter parent. My father was much more likely to show affection—to put me on his lap. Yet, I yearned for my mother's roughened hands. Sometimes I'd hide under the covers or lock myself in the bathroom because I didn't want anyone to see me cry.

I longed to show my mother everything I'd learned. I wanted her to see how I had grown. I was also worried about her. In allowing Khadija and me to live in town, she had lost two of the household's helpers. She would have to work harder to make up for our absence. The thought oppressed me. In my daydreams I saw myself bringing my mother to live in Mogadishu, buying her a house with a terrace from which she could watch the sea. When she felt like it, from time to time, she could weave a mat. But there would be nothing she absolutely had to do. She would be free at last from burdens and responsibility.

Then two years after my father had brought me to Uncle Abdulkadir's, my oldest brother Ahmed came with bad news. Our mother, who had always suffered from epilepsy, was having seizures almost daily, and her heart was weak. In the meantime our father had taken another wife. The notion of my mother being alone in her struggle with illness and competition brought tears to my eyes. I begged Uncle Abdulkadir to let me go home for the holidays. "It's a long journey and a very dangerous one. It is impossible for you to go alone. I would worry about you," he said. "And besides, I'd have to send someone out first to locate your parents."

"Please let me go to see my mother," I pleaded.

"Okay, for the holidays."

As the academic year neared its end, however, nobody talked about my journey anymore.

"Please bring my mother to Mogadishu," I begged.

"We'll see," my big brother answered.

"Next year you'll visit your mother," my uncle said. Then, with a look I didn't then understand, he added, "I'd miss you."

"You stink!"

The little daughter of the Spanish ambassador started to cry. Her sister took her by the hand. "We're circumcised too," she explained. "We were done a long time ago."

"I don't believe it," I said.

"It's true."

"Then show me!" I was the smallest but also the oldest—that was why all the girls followed my lead. We danced in a circle around the two Spanish girls. The older one looked like she'd like nothing better than to punch out my teeth. On the terrace the grown-ups were drinking tea, and from time to time the wind wafted their voices through the open windows.

"You're dirty. Ugh!" I made a face and bent down toward the younger girl. "You dribble. You're going to hell." The little one looked up, her lips trembling.

The older sister wiped her tears. "We're circumcised just like you!"

"Prove it," I commanded with the self assurance of a born leader. "Come on, let's go upstairs." The little one looked at her sister. They stalled.

"Show us! Show us!" came the chorus.

It was a showdown.

Of course, the daughters of the Spanish ambassador could have run to their parents on the terrace, but they knew what the consequences would have been the next day in school. "Okay," said the older one. The younger one said nothing.

I locked the door. "You first," I said.

"No, you," the older sister answered.

"You're chicken."

"You're chicken."

I wasn't about to stand for that. Determined, I undid the button and unzipped my jeans, hesitated for a fraction of a second, then down went the pants over my bottom and I pulled aside my panty crotch, not for long but long enough for everyone to see. One after the other all the girls did the same. Only Saïda said, "What a dumb game. I'm not playing."

Astonished, I glared at her. "It's probably because your scar isn't as beautiful as mine," I said to provoke her. Saïda simply shrugged her shoulders. "So what? It's still a stupid game."

Hurt but therefore energized, I turned to the Spanish girls. "Okay. Now it's your turn."

"No," said the big one.

"No," whispered little one.

"Saïda's right, it's a dumb game."

"You stinking drooling girl!" I shouted. "You're chicken. Or even worse: You're *not* circumcised. I'm going to tell the whole school. Tomorrow everybody's going to know you're filthy." The little one whimpered, the snot running out of her nose.

"Unless . . ." I paused, "you buy me two comic books."

"I already told you," the older girl insisted while wiping her sister's nose, "our parents had us done. We look exactly like you."

"Liar," I shouted and said to the others, "They're lying."

"Liars!" screamed the other girls. "Stinking, dirty liars."

"Get 'em. Let's look for ourselves!" As if waiting for my command, all stormed the two sisters, threw them on the bed, pressed them into the cushions, and held their arms and legs while we pulled their panties down. "I knew it," I cried. "Look at them! How wrinkled they are! How shriveled! How ugly! Yuck!"

Saïda, meanwhile, stood looking out the window as though it all had nothing to do with her.

The shoelaces fled my fingers. "Let me do that," Saïda said. "We're late." Aunt Madeleine, downstairs, was calling us, and the chauffeur had already brought the car around. My cousin knelt and tied my shoes. My fingers were simply too stiff. "I don't understand why you don't say something," Saïda reproached me. "Your fingers are horribly bent."

Without a word I shoved my arms into the sleeves of my blouse. I hid my illness from others' eyes. But I hid it from myself, as well. When others pointed it out, I felt even more depressed. I bit my lips. When the pain kept me from sleeping, I prayed, hoping that upon waking all symptoms would have vanished, and all would have faded into the landscape of bad dreams. For reasons I didn't understand, I felt guilty and did everything I could not to worry Aunt Madeleine and Uncle Abdulkadir.

In school the nuns gave us dictation. More than once the pencil slipped from my hand and clattered on the floor. Everyone looked up. I sank into my seat. Awkwardly, with my left hand, I shoved the pencil between the fingers of the right. Slowly the sister strolled between the rows, up and down. I wanted to continue writing, but the last sentence had fled from memory. At my desk the sister stopped. "Show me your notebook."

Reluctantly I presented it.

"At most you've written only half. You're not trying." She spit out the words like poison fruit. "Hold out your hands." She lifted the cane, her tone cold and threatening. I could already feel the pain, the burning. "I'm ill," I whispered.

"Your hands . . ." she repeated, as if she hadn't heard me.

"I can't move my fingers. That's why I wrote so slowly."

And suddenly rage took hold of me. "If you hit me, I'll tell my uncle. He'll arrest you."

Without warning, the rod struck. Bellowing "Your hands!" she caned my arms, my fingers, and fingertips. They burned. Everything burned. The blows continued.

In the afternoons, Uncle Abdulkadir retired to the terrace to work. Because the servants had gone out on errands, he asked me to bring him tea. I went into the kitchen and put the water on to boil. My hands were as stiff as claws so I carried the tea between my wrists. As I entered the salon, Uncle Abdulkadir looked up and asked, "What's wrong with your hands?"

The cup crashed. I fled to my room.

Uncle Abdulkadir knocked, insisting I open the door. "What's the matter with your hands?" he asked. "Have you been hurt? Did an animal bite you? Open the door and talk to me, Fadumo, I'm worried about you."

"I can't tell you anything."

"If you don't open this door, I'm going to let you have it!"

"No, you're not."

For a moment the hallway was still. In the whole house not a sound could be heard. I sniffled and wiped the tears from my eyes.

"Open the door," Uncle Abdulkadir said. "I won't hurt you."

Slowly, I opened the door. Uncle Abdulkadir examined my hands. "Why didn't I notice sooner?" he cried. "What kind of father am I?" I didn't know whether to be ashamed or proud of my success at having hidden my illness for so long.

My uncle called a doctor, a specialist from Togo who practiced in Mogadishu. The man examined my hands, finger by finger, and asked me to bend and stretch them. He felt my knees, ankles, and toes. Then he put away his instruments and shook his head: "Your daughter has rheumatism. I'm sorry, but there's nothing I can do."

4

At night I lay awake listening to the garden sounds, the meowing of roaming cats, the steady breathing of my cousins. At dawn I got up. Quietly I descended the stairs onto the terrace. On the horizon the sun appeared as a smooth peach. All my senses drank in the early light, the pink powdery color, the salty smell, the bougainvillea, the buzzing of insects in the flower beds.

The day went very quickly. With all the confusion came nervousness that spread through my chest like gas. I felt light and was close to panic, afraid I'd lose the ground beneath my feet. For days I'd eaten little.

The whole family accompanied us to the airport. The caravan proceeded onto the runway, past the loading docks, and toward the planes. I fidgeted the entire time, as if my arms and legs were obliged to translate their inner agitation into movement, to shunt it off so I wouldn't explode.

A silvery shimmer announced the plane under the sun.

"Behave yourself now," Aunt Madeleine said and embraced me. "I'm depending on you." I nodded and hugged my cousins, Ahmed and Qamaan, while Uncle Abdulkadir gave our suitcases to a worker in a blue and white uniform.

"Don't forget me," Idil called as I climbed the stairs to the plane. Everyone waved, even the nanny and the maid. I waved back.

Uncle Abdulkadir seated himself in one of the first rows. "I want to see the wings, Uncle. Can't we sit by the wings?"

"No, our places are here."

"But I want to see how the plane flies. I can't imagine how it's done. Its wings are too stiff. I saw them myself." I buzzed about at first, unable to sit still. Then a flight attendant secured my safety belt. Surprised, I looked at him but Uncle Abdulkadir nodded. With a click the buckle held. From the entrance flowed a steady stream of passengers, their luggage banging against our seats. I pressed buttons on my armrest and the light overhead went on and the seat moved. Startled, I grasped Uncle Abdulkadir's hand and held tight to the small, sky-blue pocketbook with golden clasps that Aunt Madeleine had given me.

Suddenly, there was a lurch and a groan.

A woman screamed, "Allah!"

"It's only the jet engines," Uncle Abdulkadir explained and stroked my hand. The groaning swelled and became indescribably loud. Excitement made the hairs on my arms stand on end. My uncle gave me a small paper sack just as I noticed that the airport building had started to move. Shocked I pressed my nose to the window. The plane rolled forward. Though I hardly noticed its movement, outside, people, cars, and houses slid past. The speed increased. The groaning grew louder, and we raced over the asphalt. Suddenly, there, ahead of us, the ocean opened up, but the plane remained glued to the earth. It couldn't fly after all. I knew it! We would all end up at the bottom of the sea. People screamed and prayed: "*Bismillahi Rahmani Rahim*"—Allah, protect us!

Then we took off.

The movement pinned me to the seat; my stomach seemed to rise to my chest. I leaned over, trying to find the way to open a window. I wanted to look out, to see where the earth had gone— the city, my family. I wanted to see how the stiff wings moved in order to believe what was taking place. "Sit down," Uncle Abdulkadir said. He suddenly looked quite pale. Voices continued to cry out, many of them from men who appeared composed. The flight attendant distributed moist towels and candy. She smiled as though nothing out of the ordinary were occurring.

The roar subsided and became a monotonous growl. Slowly the passengers calmed. I leaned back. Outside the sky shone as blue as the sea on tranquil days. I still held fast to Uncle Abdulkadir's hand, but I felt the weight receding and my eyes growing heavy. The humming cushioned me. Finally, I fell asleep and awoke to a sea of lights.

The plane landed in Rome behind schedule. As we walked through the sliding door into the airport, I felt as though someone had tossed me into a turbulent sea. Millions of people seemed to be shouting, yelling, shrieking.

And all of them looked like Signor Lavera.

Instantly his picture appeared before my eyes: Signor Lavera, an Italian textile manufacturer, who had visited my uncle one evening. I had come home from school and gone out on the terrace—and suddenly found myself facing a man whose look could have turned you to stone. Only gradually did the shock melt: Normally I would have approached this person with the vigilance reserved for dangerous predators. Cautiously, I touched his arm and stroked his skin. "Are you ill?" I asked, my voice choked with sympathy.

"Stop it!" my uncle said sternly. "Behave yourself."

But the guest laughed. "What makes you think so?" he asked.

"Because you look like the garbage man. And he's albino, Aunt Madeleine said. That's why she always gives him a cream for his skin." Signor Lavera held his stomach as he laughed. My uncle appeared both moved and embarrassed.

"I'm Italian," Signor Lavara explained. "In Italy everyone looks like me. Well . . ." He had been fumbling with his hair and I couldn't resist the temptation to touch it as well. It felt like fur, smooth and thick. "Not everyone has red hair and green eyes, but everyone's light skinned."

Signor Lavera hadn't lied.

"Give me your hand," said Uncle Abdulkadir and pushed me

through the crowd while I remained openmouthed in wonder. As we passed a man in uniform, I stopped. Never had I seen such sky-blue eyes! The man looked at me, quizzically at first, and then, laughing, bent down and gave my cheek a playful pinch. I felt angry. I wanted to pinch him back, but Uncle Abdulkadir pulled me along.

We left the foyer and entered a long corridor. It was cold. I was freezing in a light blue pantsuit even though Aunt Madeleine had asked the tailor to make three layers of lining, one on top of the other. It was still too thin. In Mogadishu, there was nowhere to buy a coat. When he saw two women in Somali dress and sandals, Uncle Abdulkadir shook his head. "Country folk," he complained. "How can they be so ignorant? What will the Italians think of us Somalis?" To me, the women didn't appear to be dressed out of the ordinary. How were they supposed to know that in Italy they'd draw attention to themselves? How could they possibly anticipate such cold? The air felt as though you were inside our German refrigerator.

At customs, uniformed men looked at our passports. Some documents were handed right back with a nod, while others were retained and thoroughly thumbed through, observed with stern, tight expressions. My passport was among those carefully studied. Were they aware that twelve-year-old Somali girls couldn't yet obtain a passport? Did they know that my uncle had had to print one for me in his shop?

Uncle Abdulkadir led me toward the stairs. Voices echoed from the ceiling, though I couldn't identify who was speaking. Again my breathing stopped. The stairway was moving! It moved and disappeared right in front of me into the earth. A stairway that emerged from nothing and went back to nothing! Uncle Abdulka-dir grasped my hand. "That's an escalator. It moves so you don't have to climb." I had to laugh. Never had I heard a grown-up say a sillier thing.

But I refused to set foot on the step.

Behind us people began piling up, pushing us aside, rushing

past. On the next escalator a Somali woman screamed for help. The mechanism had trapped her wraparound. My uncle threatened and pleaded with me. Then a strange woman took my hand, placed it on the rubber banister and gently pushed me after it. "Just hold on tight," she said in English. She was pretty and smelled warm and flowery. Without being able to do anything about it, I was carried by the staircase into the air.

At the top I collided with a soft and massive fat man, seemingly planted there for me to bang directly into. As I teetered, he reached for my arm, bent down, and wordlessly looked at me. His expression frightened me. The man raised his finger, licked its tip, and rubbed it across my cheek. I was so surprised that I forgot to breathe.

"You racist!" I heard Uncle Abdulkadir shout. The man answered with a resounding laugh. My uncle grabbed me and pulled me away, walking so fast that I stumbled. The man yelled after us, but I didn't understand his language. Suitcases banged against my legs, and handbags bumped my head. I tried to dodge the crowd, running around and between people. All of them— men, women, children—were pale-skinned, some also white haired. Like the fat man, I wondered if the color would come off if I rubbed it.

In the taxi I pressed my nose against the window. Here, too, streets were chaotic and noisy. "Leave me alone already about the Italians," a great aunt of mine had yelled when she heard I'd be going to a hospital in Rome. "When they were in Somalia, they paved the streets with Somalis so they wouldn't have to dirty their shoes."

So this was the country to which I had come.

Uncle Omar, Uncle Abdulkadir's brother, was secretary to the ambassador in Rome and lived in a house so tall that it seemed to touch the sky. The elevator took us to the fourteenth floor where we rang the bell.

My sister Khadija opened the door.

We fell into each other's arms, laughing and crying, hugging and kissing. We couldn't let each other go. Since that night when Khadija had run away from the old man she was supposed to marry, we hadn't seen each other. No one knew that she had taken refuge with Uncle Omar.

I could not stop looking at her. Khadija had inherited our mother's round, soft face, her dark skin and even teeth. I felt as though I were seeing both of them at the same time.

That night I crept into Khadija's bed and we talked until dawn. Before I fell asleep, I could swear my mother's aroma of herbs and earth had filled my nostrils.

In the hospital I found myself in a room with fifty other patients. Whenever a physician came, a nurse followed with a portable screen set up around the bed of the patient he was visiting.

Every day a doctor appeared. He would stroke my head and say, "*Buon giorno.* Did you get a good night's sleep?" I would nod. He would take my blood pressure and feel my pulse, ask me to stick out my tongue, and look toward the ceiling so that he might look at my eyeballs. He'd knock on my chest and back, tell me to breathe in, breathe out, and hold.

That was it.

At the end of the first week I had made friends with some of the other patients and nurses. None looked like monsters or people who would plaster streets with Somalis so they wouldn't dirty their shoes. Instead, all of them were worried about and shocked to see my emaciated frame. The nurses tried to take good care of me and fatten me up. At home, I'd be content with a bowl of rice for my evening meal, and while the others were busy eating, I'd hide a mound of food in a drawer of the table. I was simply not hungry, and whenever anyone tried to convince me to eat, I ate even less. Here, where we had pasta every day, I soon discovered that the older women in the room were happy to receive part of my portion.

At the end of the second week Uncle Abdulkadir returned to Mogadishu. Khadija came to see me as often as she could, and I impatiently awaited her visits. As children we'd fought because she had been my rival, and I had wanted to prove that I was more clever and prettier than she. Khadija had been a willful child, hot tempered, who could run really fast. But she was also a coward who screamed whenever she saw a snake. I was always ready to place a dead serpent on her wraparound and yell, "Khadija! Watch out for the poisonous snake. Don't move!" Later, she would exact her revenge, and I would run to our mother to tell on her—this was an endless cycle. Now that we were far from home and older, we became close friends.

She worked as a maid for Uncle Omar. On the day I had entered the hospital, he had beaten her because she had broken a fine porcelain cup. Uncle Abdulkadir would never have done that! Our lives had unfolded differently, because we had been placed in the care of two quite different men. While I had been sent to school to become an educated person, Khadija had been treated as a slave. She could not read or write.

From time to time, Uncle Omar looked in on me. "Are you in pain?" he asked. I nodded.

"Are they giving you something for it?" I shook my head.

Immediately he summoned a doctor to my bedside. "Heal the girl," my uncle said. "She's been here for four weeks. Make sure she's finally given the help she needs!" Then he disappeared back to the embassy.

For hours I lay in bed staring at the ceiling and at the brown water spots on the dirty floor until they took shape as figures and faces that became characters in stories. I felt abandoned and lonely and bored. Since I was spending a lot of time flat on my back, the pain in my joints faded. The deformity of my fingers and toes, however, remained. Some of my toes had stopped growing altogether so that, side by side, they were of various lengths. I constantly prayed and hoped that at some point, suddenly, it would all be over and behind me—that I'd have pretty hands and feet again. In the meantime, the doctor stroked my head, took my blood pressure, felt my pulse, knocked on my chest and back, and told me to breathe in, breathe out, and hold.

"In three months nothing has happened," Uncle Omar scolded. "The girl can get the same treatment in Somalia. And there she wouldn't even have to miss school!"

A few days later another doctor announced that defective nerves might have been causing the problem. He wanted to test the theory with electroshock therapy. A nurse buckled me in so I couldn't move during the procedure. A physician used needles to puncture me at various points along my spine and in my shoulders and knees. I almost shrieked the soul out of my body. Finally, Uncle Omar put an end to the torture. Obviously, my nerves were sensitive and intact, and the doctors were unable to cure my rheumatism.

Without any further explanation I was discharged.

Screaming I bolted upright, bathed in sweat and shaking. A voice in the night carried from somewhere far away, scarcely reaching my ear. Very slowly I was able to identify the voice as Khadija's. She was calling my name. Now I saw her face, saw her next to me, felt her hands on my body. "Shhh—" She pulled my head to her breast.

My body heaved. I cried without respite, my teeth clenched hard. I had been dreaming, and in the dream I had begun to cry. Once again I felt the electric shock in all my limbs, but I couldn't visualize what was happening. My sister whispered, "It'll be all right," and gently stroked my hair. She repeated my name like a mantra.

"I have a stomachache," I sobbed. "It hurts so much."

"It'll be all right," Khadija said again. I let myself sink onto her soft breast and threw my arms around my own body, holding myself tight and letting myself be held by her as well. My sobbing grew quieter, the fright faded, and the quivering—the evil shocks—drew back like a wave. Then they gathered strength and in the next moment reared and broke over me again. I collapsed under the deluge. I cried and screamed, "Mommy!"

A few weeks later Uncle Omar was transferred from the embassy in Rome to Kenya. The family started to pack, and I packed as well. Uncle Omar flew out first to look for a house to rent in Nairobi.

I often saw Khadija crying, but when I asked what was wrong, she always said she'd been peeling onions and it didn't matter.

A few days before the planned departure my aunt told me I wouldn't be going with them. "You're going to Germany. Your uncle has arranged everything."

Uncle Abdulkadir had asked a friend who owed him a favor and worked in the Somali embassy in Bonn to look after me. Someone would pick me up at the airport. Until treatment began I could stay with him and his family. As soon as a hospital bed became free, I'd go to a special clinic near Bonn.

There they would cure my illness.

With a sign hanging around my neck I landed at the Cologne-Bonn airport. A flight attendant put me in the care of another air-line employee, who took me to a waiting area. She said something I didn't understand and disappeared. With my little suitcase in hand I stood there, petrified with fear. People hurried past. They seemed to be fighting with one another, their language sounded so harsh. Nobody smiled. It was colder here than in Italy.

Nobody came to get me.

After some time two men approached. They were in uniform and carried pistols on their hips. One of them leaned down and said something to me. The other gestured toward my suitcase. I grabbed it and ran like the devil all the way down the corridor, sprinting as fast as I could, but the suitcase was suddenly heavy. It banged against my legs, and dragged on the floor. The men chased after me. One of them called out, and then they caught up with me. One man held me by my shoulder and arm. The other took the suitcase. I screamed and twisted out of their reach. I tripped, and the suitcase fell with a loud bang, the locks gave way and all my poor possessions flew across the stone tiles. Tears filled my eyes. One of the policemen laughed. The other one bent down and gathered up my things. I picked up a blouse and underpants, tore a skirt and a nightshirt out of the stranger's hands. I tried to salvage whatever I could.

Then a voice called my name.

A man in a uniform presented himself as the chauffeur of His Excellency the Somali Ambassador. I would have liked to scream at him, Why come now? Why had I been waiting alone among fearsome foreigners? But I said nothing, closed my suitcase, and trailed after him. He led me to a black Mercedes. Relieved, I sank into the back seat. Leather crunched, and I detected the weak, sharp smell of motor oil, recognizing luxury. At last, here was something familiar.

Without a word, the chauffeur drove the limousine through the streets. I was surprised to see so clean a road and a swept sidewalk. Even the trees were tidier than in Italy. Everyone seemed to move with purpose. An uncle in Mogadishu had told me that the Germans were good people, especially Hitler because he had passed laws to do something about the Jews. For that reason my uncle named one of his sons Hitler, and Hitler and I sometimes used to play catch together.

We stopped in front of a villa surrounded by high trees. They looked like dark figures someone had left behind and forgotten. There was something desolate about the house and garden. The chauffeur carried my suitcase up the stairs and pressed a black button. The sky was raining ice. I was freezing. The metal door opened, and a maid appeared. Without a word she drew me inside.

The house was spacious. At the far end of the foyer a stairway led to the upper stories. On the left you could see through an open double door into a salon. I heard voices. We climbed the stairs, and the maid knocked on a door. After a few seconds someone called out, "Come in." In front of a vanity sat an older woman wearing an elegant bathrobe and removing rollers from her hair. I recognized her as one of Aunt Madeleine's friends. Some time had elapsed since we had seen each other in Mogadishu. I greeted her, and since it was hard to gauge the meaning of the look she gave me, I added, "I'm the daughter of Uncle Abdulkadir."

"Hm," said the woman and pulled a hairpin out of a roller. I felt unwelcome. She reached for a comb and continued to do her hair, giving orders to the maid in a foreign language. She took my measure and murmured at last, "We have guests. But the girl can certainly find some place to sleep."

They put me in a room at the end of the hallway in which four children were already sleeping. Several mattresses lay on the floor. When I asked in which closet I could hang my things, the woman answered, "There's no point in unpacking. You won't be staying long."

During the days that followed, I lived in an atmosphere of similar cold indifference. No one showed an interest in me and nobody talked to me. When they did I was spoken to as if I were a beggar. I was told that I belonged to another tribe, and that my family was not well respected. I felt as though I had been hit on the head. In Mogadishu, this ambassador and his wife had been friends of Uncle Abdulkadir and Aunt Madeleine. They had visited, and we had gone out together to eat and celebrate. Here they accused me of stealing: A golden amulet disappeared and the wife of the ambassador stormed into my room, ripped open my trunk, and rummaged around in it, while the rest of the family watched. "I don't need to steal," I shouted, enraged. "I own jewelry. My family gave me lots of gold."

Not finding the amulet only heightened the ambassador's wife's suspicion. "You've buried it in order to wear it later," she hissed. "Tell me where you've hidden it!" Her son hit me while the other children shouted curses. Sick and unwanted, I threw a blanket over myself. On a mattress on a floor in a foreign country, I cried myself to sleep.

The only one who had a kind word for me was Irina, the Russian cook. She had been working in the Somali embassy for quite some time and had seen a number of ambassadors come and go. She confided to me that the current one wasn't her favorite. Irina spoke a little Somali, and I often chatted with her in the kitchen, watching her prepare dinner for the fat, spoiled children of the embassy.

The chauffeur drove me to the clinic. At the end of the entrance he stopped, got out, and placed my suitcase on the pebbles. I asked him to help me carry it into the foyer. He hesitated. Without a word—but angry—I exhibited my deformed fingers.

At the reception desk a nurse greeted me. When she noticed that I didn't speak German, she tried English. My uncle had already taken care of all the admission formalities, so they had been waiting for me. "Come," she said, taking my suitcase and my hand. "I'll show you to your room."

Like a good little girl, I followed her. "I'm Nurse Ute," she said. She was a slim-bodied woman with very long, soft hair. Whenever she laughed, dimples appeared around her mouth. But what fascinated me most were her trousers. They were even tighter than Saïda's bleached jeans or my own. Now she pressed a button on the wall. A door sprang open and we entered a broad corridor with green doors on either side. In front of one sat a man on a chair much too small for him. As we went by, he looked up with anticipation. Nurse Ute shook her head and said, "I'm sorry, but we don't have any news." The man sank back. We entered a second corridor where this time the doors were blue.

"Here it is," Nurse Ute announced and knocked on one of the doors. I entered a spacious room with two beds. One was empty and the other was occupied by a boy who appeared to be sleeping. A thin ribbon of saliva ran from his mouth. Dusky light filtered through the windows, and I would have liked to pull back the curtains and look out. "Shall we put your things in the dresser?" Nurse Ute asked. "Would you like me to help?"

During the next few days I was examined by a professor and a few other doctors. They measured and weighed me. Again everyone was horrified at my weight. They took blood, administered EKGs and EEGs, and x-rayed me. At last the professor confirmed the Togolese clinician's diagnosis: I suffered from rheumatism. My hands and feet, as well as my knees and hips, were already degenerating because of the illness. My hands and feet had suffered the most advanced bone damage. The professor told me, "That can neither be changed nor stopped." In one quick sentence, he dashed my dreams of recovery. I was devastated. "The only thing we can do is delay progress of the disease."

The doctors prescribed physical therapy, cold and heat treatments, as well as massage. I had to learn to swim in the clinic's pool. Because I was too proud to admit that I could not swim, I sank like a stone to the bottom the first time the instructor let go of me. From then on I paddled with a rubber tube around my waist. And every second afternoon a sports therapist would play tennis with me. The nurses stuffed me with vitamins. In addition to those, I was also taking medicine. At breakfast I swallowed three tablets and in the afternoon, a few more. When I added them all up in the evening, I found I was taking nine pills a day.

That alone satisfied my hunger.

But then something extraordinary occurred. Suddenly I began to eat again. I had breakfast. At noon I ate chicken, two servings of yogurt, and a chocolate bar for dessert—and two hours later I would be hungry again. My body fleshed out quickly and my weight doubled. My pants and T-shirts became too tight and pretty soon my legs rubbed against each other when I walked. Then my skin began to break. No one had told me to use skin cream. No one had noticed that—unaccustomed to the moist, cold German climate—I continued to shower three times a day as I had done in Mogadishu. Finally, Nurse Ute noticed that something was amiss. "Doesn't your family visit?" she asked.

I shook my head. Neither the ambassador nor his wife had ever come. I had spent one weekend with them, but they didn't have a mattress for me anymore. I had asked the ambassador's wife for money to buy a new T-shirt, but she had scoffed, "Do I look like the Bank of England?" I then watched her hand her daughter a 100 deutsche mark bill. When they took away the blanket I had borrowed to sleep under on the sofa and told me to use a towel instead, I decided not to return. The next morning Nurse Ute pulled a skirt, blouse, and sandals out of a paper bag. "Get dressed," she said. "We're going to town." We returned with new gym shoes, trousers, a matching pullover, several T-shirts and underpants. I never learned where the money had come from. Had Uncle Abdulkadir transferred it, or had Nurse Ute dressed me out of her own pocket?

I woke up with a stomachache. During the day it worsened. Something was ripping and tearing in there. My back hurt. When I went to the toilet at noon I found blood on my underpants. With shaking fingers I cleaned myself and washed the panties. Two hours later a large stain appeared on my jeans. Crying I ran to the toilet. Like a ghost, the excisor suddenly appeared before me—her crippled fingers, the clearing, the thorns. I didn't know what it was, but clearly something in me had broken. They were going to have to sew me up a second time! Fear grabbed me by the throat. What had I done wrong? Was I pregnant? But I'd never had sex! Would I have a child?

In any event, it was my fault. That much was clear.

I ran through the halls. Once back in the room I collided with Nurse Ute, who was distributing medicine. "Why are you crying?" she asked. I was ashamed of myself, but greater than that shame were fear and despair. I told her about the blood on my panties. "That's nothing to worry about," Nurse Ute said with a friendly smile, wiping the tears from my cheeks. "Now you're a woman." She told me what I needed to know, gave me a sanitary napkin, and something to take for the pain. A few days later the bleeding stopped and the stomachache vanished.

For many months I was busy with my rheumatism therapy program. The pain in my joints faded and they stopped swelling despite pressure on them. I could hardly believe the prognosis of the professor. Maybe my illness really was curable? I talked myself into optimism even as I encouraged the boy in my room who had cerebral palsy. "You can walk!" I said to him when I sat at his bedside at night. "You only have to want to!" As a nomadic child I knew how important persistence and willpower were. "And stop drooling."

One Friday afternoon, I wandered aimlessly through town. Nurse Ute had invited me to her apartment, but I had declined because I had spent the preceding weekend with her and I didn't want to wear out my welcome. In front of city hall I sat on the edge of a fountain and closed my eyes. The stone had been warmed by the sun. It took a moment before I realized that a voice was talking to me. A man in black leather pants stood there. He wore a vest and had a bandana tied around his forehead. His rustic boots made me think about how sweaty his feet must be feeling. His glance was interested—neither friendly nor aggressive. "What is an African girl doing in Bonn?" he repeated.

"I live here," was my answer.

"Really? Where?"

I hesitated before saying, "With the ambassador from Somalia."

"Hm." He rubbed his beard, turned, spun back, and remained silent. I wondered whether my answer had impressed him. Just as I was on the point of inquiring where he lived, he asked, "Would you like to go for a ride on my motorcycle?"

I nodded. "Sure."

He gestured in the direction of the parking lot. There stood a big black bike. "By the way, my name is Peter."

I climbed aboard, and we headed out along the old post road. The wind pulled at my T-shirt but I felt warm, comfortable, and refreshed. I had never been on a motorcycle before. A bit fearful, I held firmly on to Peter and took care to keep my feet from sliding off the rests. We left the old city behind, slipping onto a country road that wove through cornfields and meadows. Peter asked if he was driving too fast. I told him everything was fine, but as soon as the bike entered a curve, my stomach lurched.

Peter veered from the country road into a dirt lane. As we bounced, I held on more tightly. A hanging branch touched my helmet, making a strange sound. I had no idea where we were going.

"We're meeting a couple of friends at the lake," Peter explained. I nodded, as though I had known all along.

On the shore we found half a dozen other bikes. Their owners were lying on the grass drinking beer. Everyone was astonished to see me. Somebody asked: "Who's that?"

"Fadumo," Peter answered. "She lives at the ambassador's." Everyone was impressed. One of the bikers sat up and asked, "Which one?"

"The Somali ambassador," I replied.

"You're from Somalia?" asked another.

"Yes," I said.

"Where is Somalia anyway?" Peter asked, taking a beer.

We communicated in a hodgepodge of English, German, Italian, and Somali. As evening approached, someone made a campfire. Someone else pulled a plastic sack filled with hot dogs out of the water. Peter speared one on a twig and offered it to me; like the others, I held it over the crackling fire and let it brown. Someone rolled a cigarette, lit up, took a drag, then passed it on. The tobacco smelled sweet. When I got tired, Peter gave me a sleeping bag. I slipped inside and watched the stars, so thick overhead I felt as if I could grab one. I wondered how long it had been since I'd slept out in the open. To the sound of soft music, their voices, and the crackle of burning wood, I fell asleep.

I spent a whole week with the bikers. During the day we rode motorcycles. Once I even fell asleep while moving and almost fell off. Toward evening someone would manage to get something to eat. We set up camp in empty houses, on lakeshores, or in meadows. Sometimes different bikers joined us or a couple of biker girls, but most of the time Peter, his friends, and I were alone. They treated me as if I were a princess. And I felt good being with them. This life was different from anything I had yet experienced. One day the leader of the group asked me, "What's with your ambassador? Isn't he out looking for you?"

The next day Peter drove me back to Bonn.

In the hospital I ran right into Nurse Ute's arms. "Where were you?" She had been beside herself with worry. I had thought no one would notice my absence, and in fact, at first that was the case. People at the hospital thought I was at the ambassador's. But when I missed my usual treatments, Nurse Ute began to ask questions. She called the embassy, where everyone had assumed I was at the hospital. Worry increased when Uncle Abdulkadir arrived in Bonn and announced that he'd come for his daughter. I felt very guilty to have caused the few people who cared about me so much worry.

"I'm so sorry, Nurse Ute," I said.

By way of reply, she told me to "sit down on that chair and don't move." Then she went next door and used the telephone.

"Let's get your things," Nurse Ute said when she came back. Suddenly, I felt frightened. On no account did I want to return to the ambassador's house.

"I'll go only if you come, too," I wailed and used both arms to block her way.

"Yes, I'm going to drive you. Your uncle is already waiting."

When Nurse Ute's sky-blue Beetle rattled up the driveway, I could see Uncle Abdulkadir on the steps. The car had hardly pulled to a stop before I ripped open the door and fell into his arms. Then everything—all the meanness and insults and loneliness—broke from me in a torrent. Uncle Abdulkadir asked no questions. We didn't even reenter the house to take leave of the ambassador and his wife.

We went to a hotel. Uncle Abdulkadir bought me new clothes and took me to a hairdresser. We bought presents for our family. I found fabric for my mother, along with creams and oils, perfumes and jewelry. Uncle Abdulkadir watched me, laughing, but also seeming somehow depressed. I asked if I had chosen too many gifts. "No, child," he answered. "Buy whatever you like."

The next morning we drove to the hospital for one last examination. Uncle Abdulkadir paid the bill. The doctors ordered me to continue the exercises and gave me some medicine.

From the clinic we took a taxi to the airport.

5

Mogadishu now seemed dusty and provincial to me. People hurried by, few properly dressed, and many without shoes. The air vibrated with noises and smells. I was no longer used to the confusion. I whisked a fly from my hand and wondered how a country could be so chaotic.

The family picked us up at the airport. My cousins would have liked nothing better than to open all my suitcases and bags bursting with gifts on the spot. But I kept them for later, exploiting my position and acting as if I had been treated as a princess while I was away. Her Majesty was returning home to bestow her largesse on the underlings. It wasn't long before my cousins picked a fight. "Fatso," Saïda bluffed and turned away. Up until that moment, she had only ever called me "beanpole" when she was upset with me.

In my absence the house had been transformed into a real palace. I almost didn't recognize it.

Everywhere you looked there was luxury and splendor. "Unpack already!" Idil urged. Patronizingly I let the locks on my suitcases snap open. After everybody had received their gifts, I removed a golden pot and said, "Look. This cream is for my mother." I offered Idil the little jar so she could admire it. "Uncle Abdulkadir let me buy so many gifts! During the coming holidays I'll certainly be able to visit my parents."

Idil turned to stone with the jar in her hand. Saïda looked at me aghast. "But your mother is dead," she said. "Don't you know?"

A cold hand reached into my bowels and ripped out all my strength. Fear slid in. "How can you say such a thing?" I asked softly. "How can you be so mean? Why do you want my mother to die? Why do you have such evil thoughts? What did I ever do to you? I curse you!" Enraged, I threw a shoe at my cousin.

"It's true," Saïda yelled. "Your mother has been dead for months!" The door slammed behind her.

No sound escaped me.

Icy pain ran down my spine.

My heart seemed to stop beating.

In the afternoon my brothers, Ahmed and Jama, came. I didn't want to talk to anyone. I lay in the garden under a tree, like an insect's empty carapace, my body drained of life even though my eyes could see, and my lungs breathe.

I couldn't believe that my mother was dead.

I couldn't believe they'd lied to me for so long.

I couldn't even cry.

Uncle Abdulkadir came late in the afternoon. He sat down next to me, and for a long time neither of us said a word. He simply put his arm around my shoulders. At some point I noticed that he was crying. "I didn't want to burden you. You were so cheerful in Bonn. You looked so good among all those presents—so happy. I simply couldn't do it."

"You let me run straight into heartbreak."

"I only wanted to protect you, daughter." He pressed me to him. "You weren't supposed to hear about it like that."

My legs were like cotton wads, my head a helium balloon.

The world wobbled.

Pain alone kept me on earth.

"I don't want anything more to do with any of you." I stood up. My body was feather light, and yet every movement was heavy, as though some force were pulling on each limb. Such breathtaking emptiness. They had passed me from one family to the next. And the only person to whom I felt deeply inseparable had died.

What meaning did life have now?

I went into the bathroom, filled a glass with water, and swallowed all the pills in my luggage.

They pumped my stomach.

Mechanically, like a puppet, I moved through the days that followed. I obeyed if someone ordered me to do something, took care of what needed to be done. The longing I felt for my mother gave way to the pain gnawing at my body.

I trusted no one anymore, not even Uncle Abdulkadir. At first he knocked on my door and tried to sit with me. But I turned him away. Then he forced me to listen, so I did, but his words failed to reach me. They slid down the thick rubber wall I had built around myself.

Every night I saw my mother in my dreams. I saw her on the steppe at the fence of our compound. Her left hand on her hip, she waved to my father and me. My mother had died on that night when I was in Rome, dreaming of her. With her I lost a chunk of home.

I hated everyone who forced me to remain alive.

I stopped eating.

At some point Uncle Abdulkadir drew away from me. He and Aunt Madeleine fought more and more often. At night I heard their voices and sometimes the sound of slamming doors. Some of Aunt Madeleine's relatives visited, and no sooner had they gone than relatives of Uncle Abdulkadir took their place. If representatives of both families found themselves face-to-face, a quarrel was inevitable. Uncle Abdulkadir felt under pressure to behave as a proper Somali, not a European. Before, such pressures had united the couple. But now I heard my uncle forbidding his wife to travel to Djibouti and London. He threatened to sell her car. It was unseemly, he said, for a woman to drive. Aunt Madeleine defended herself and screamed at him. I held my ears. Their quarrels frightened me. Never before had Uncle Abdulkadir told his wife what to do. On the contrary, he had urged her to enjoy her freedom and to be independent, and he had defended her against all criticism. Something very basic had changed, but I couldn't figure it out.

Days passed in which Aunt Madeleine spoke to no one. She rejected me outright, as if she had never wanted me in her house. She hardly left her room. The servants neglected their work, weeds sprouted in the garden, the flowers dried up, and the pools remained empty. It was unthinkable! The house was dirty. Watching everything fall apart made me very sad. I closed my eyes, listened to music, and dreamed myself miles away. I hoped that robbers would break in, steal everything, murder us all, and put an end to life. In school, I had trouble following the lessons. Languages collided in my head. If someone spoke to me in Arabic or Somali, I answered in German or Italian, sometimes even in English. At night I lay awake listening to the stray cats meowing out their passions. I cried and wished fervently that everything were as it had been before.

Relatives told me that my father's new wife let my little brother Muhammad go hungry. I begged Ahmed and Jama to bring Muhammad to Mogadishu. But nothing happened. One afternoon I found a pistol in Uncle Abdulkadir's study. I looked at it and picked it up. I held it against my temple. I was afraid to pull the trigger. And anyway, I didn't know whether it was loaded.

Then Aunt Madeleine got pregnant.

For a couple of months life actually became what it had been before I'd left for Europe. There were invitations and parties, and my cousins and I served at receptions. But scarcely had little Husen been born than the fights began again, and this time worse than ever.

Again I experienced the tearing, the fist in my stomach, a pulling, a twisting—blood and cramps. With my belly like lead, I threw up for days on end. My back ached, and I limped, bent over, like an old woman. This time was much worse than in Germany; I had no one to support me in Mogadishu.

It lasted for fourteen days.

The next month brought the same pain, the same nausea. The blood seeped out of the tiny opening much too slowly, sometimes blocked by clots. The pain was much more intense than when I urinated. But I didn't tell my cousins. I was suffering from something unspeakable.

Again it lasted for fourteen days.

Hardly had one period passed than I began to fear the next. Half my life was filled with pain; the other half, fear of pain. Every time I menstruated, a monster played havoc with my inner organs, twisting them inside out. No medicine worked. If I made it to school, they sent me home. Suddenly I understood the high absentee rate among nearly all the girls.

Finally Aunt Madeleine noticed that I had started my periods. She gave me hand towels to use because sanitary napkins were not available. And she advised me, at the first signs, to do some sports, to go swimming, to exercise, and to put a hot water bottle on my stomach. That would weaken the cramps. Aunt Madeleine suffered with me, and for a moment I felt the old trust. What I didn't understand was why Saïda complained only of minor bellyaches during her periods.

At some point Uncle Abdulkadir took notice of what was going on. He grumbled about antiquated traditions and barbaric rites. "To hell with the witches," he cried. "These excisors don't know what they're doing to young girls." Pinned to the ground with cramps and pain, I felt better, hearing my uncle curse the excisors. I joined him in his reproaches, every single day.

"If you'd only come to us sooner," Aunt Madeleine said, "you would have been saved." Nobody talked about it, but I began to suspect that Aunt Madeline was not circumcised and that she had spared her daughters.

Somalia has always been a country governed by clans. President Siad Barre, who had once advocated a socialist society and had said he opposed tribal rule and nepotism, felt he was under political pressure. Soon he had filled all key positions in politics and the economy with members of his clan and mine, the Marehans. Not surprisingly, members of other clans were not pleased.

At the same time, the regime failed to deal with the conflict between northerners and southerners, or to combat growing unemployment and the loss of educated Somalis. The military drained funds away from schools. Government-controlled enterprises proved increasingly unprofitable. Then beginning in 1977 Somalia fought Ethiopia over control of Ogaden, a region on the border. When the Somali army was routed, more than a million refugees fled. Although Somalia broke with the Soviet Union, the West did not offer the hoped for funds or military support. In terms of domestic and foreign policy, by 1978 Somalia was in crisis, its population in turmoil. In April 1978 a group of officers tried to oust the president, but the coup d'état failed.

The regime reacted with more repression.

On both sides of the promenade, soldiers stood at attention. They wore spats, carried white nightsticks, and suffered the heat under metal helmets. With their rifles shouldered, they sweated under the sun, the golden buttons on their uniforms twinkling. Idil fanned air my way. The bleachers heaved with tension. The crowd ignored the soldiers. People pushed and shoved, trying to make room for themselves. Lined up to march were the leaders of the various clans that now comprised the administration. Ordinary people had to remain behind the barriers and would have to enjoy the May 1 parade from there. Over our heads—heavy and stiff—hung the Somali national flag.

Suddenly police approached us, the chief speaking in earnest tones to Uncle Abdulkadir. He rose immediately and signaled us to follow the police. Rapidly we were escorted through the crowd. The bomb went off after the military parade had already begun, at that exact spot where my family had been standing moments before.

A month later, arsonists burned our school. Only property was damaged. No one was hurt. On the street, people avoided us.

Wherever Uncle Abdulkadir's car appeared, people showed their fear. Children with whom my cousins and I had played kept away from us. Their parents forbade any contact. One day a boy said, "You're oppressors of the people. We don't want anything more to do with you."

Siad Barre was my uncle; his grandfather and my great-grand-father had been brothers. There were times when Uncle Siad had visited Uncle Abdulkadir. To us he had seemed strange because he always wore dark glasses that made him look like a mafioso. But he was friendly to us. In the war against Ethiopia he had sent his own sons to the front as if he were saying, Look, I'm just like you. That impressed me, and I was shocked that people were now criticizing him. In foreign newspapers I read that the president was a dictator. Nobody told me what that meant. Although my family and the administration were in close contact, at home we never discussed politics. But in the streets I felt the dissatisfaction and unrest increasing daily.

It was too much for me, and I fell ill. The fever came on suddenly, and with it the shivers. My whole body ached, and everything I tried to eat tasted bitter as gall, so I threw it up. Aunt Madeleine and Uncle Abdulkadir had just left for a European tour in a last effort to save their marriage. They had left us in the care of the servants and a relative of Aunt Madeleine. When my temperature topped 104 degrees Fahrenheit, the nanny phoned the relative, pleading with her to come and bring a doctor, since she was the one in charge of our money. But she merely answered that I would recover on my own.

The nanny did everything she could think of to bring down the fever. When the relative finally sent for a doctor, the physician diagnosed malaria and gave me infusions to stop my dehydration. When Aunt Madeleine and Uncle Abdulkadir returned, my condition was no longer life threatening, but they found me no more than skin and bone. Uncle Abdulkadir's distress was written on his face when he saw me, and I felt guilty.

No sooner had I recovered than my rheumatism broke out

again. My joints swelled to many times their normal size. On many days both legs were swollen from the hips to the feet and I couldn't even go to the toilet by myself. The nanny provided me with hot water bottles. Uncle Abdulkadir ordered medicine. But my joints stayed stiff. Then I got asthma and stopped growing. Still I went to school. I was obsessed with preparing for final exams. I studied hard and couldn't have cared less when Idil and Saïda teased me for being a grind. Somehow I understood that, someday, I'd be empty-handed. All I might have to depend on would be my education.

No sooner had I passed the exam than Uncle Abdulkadir and Aunt Madeleine decided to separate. They sent me back to Germany.

In Germany

6

Small as a matchbox, the apartment, on the third floor of a student residence, contained a cooking corner and a shower. Sahra, a cousin of Aunt Madeleine, lived there with her brother Jamal and stepson, Rashid. "German doctors are the best," Uncle Abdulkadir had declared. Besides, I'd be better off with relatives than with strangers.

That's how I got to Munich.

Suddenly I was living in a very small space. The four of us slept together in a single bed. That didn't bother me. I was happy to have left my crisis-ridden home behind. A change of air seemed to help my rheumatism, and pretty soon I was almost free of pain. Jamal, who was there on scholarship studying electrical engineering, used his contacts and visited the appropriate offices to apply for a larger apartment. German law allowed family members to follow resident spouses, and he claimed I was his wife. Thus we were able to move to a three-room social welfare flat. I was always shocked whenever Jamal would say—in earnest or in jest—that we were married.

Sahra's husband, Ibrahim, lived in Berlin. A doctor of veterinary science, he had finished first in his class, yet as a black vet, Berlin was the only place he could find work. Rashid, his son, had come to Germany after physicians had diagnosed polio. His right leg was shorter than his left. The boy underwent many operations as surgeons tried to lengthen his leg. Eventually he was fitted for a prosthesis which had to be altered every time he grew. Nonetheless, Rashid was a cheerful boy.

In the new apartment Jamal claimed a room for himself. Sahra, Rashid, and I shared the other bedroom. Then Sahra invited her grandmother to live with us. Madame La Lune, a woman more than eighty years old, had lived for many years in France. She was very fond of gin. Finally, when Ibrahim came back from Berlin to try once more to find employment near his family, space became even tighter. Ibrahim also took me to the university clinic.

There a professor of hand surgery examined my twisted fingers. He bent them, twisted them, measured them, and took x-rays. He spoke to Ibrahim, who nodded enthusiastically, while I sat there not understanding a word. Finally, the two men shook hands. "The professor is going to operate," Ibrahim said as we took the streetcar home. "He's going to straighten your fingers." It seemed so easy and permanent. In only a few weeks I'd have pretty, straight hands! I was numb with pleasure.

The operation took place several days later.

I woke up with a plaster cast on my right arm. In the afternoon the professor came, and, this time, Ibrahim translated. Into the middle knuckle of each finger they had inserted metal rods, which would be removed in six weeks. Impatient, I longed for the day.

When it finally arrived the nurse took off the plaster, and I saw a thin, gray hand with fingers that appeared unnaturally long. The tight bandage had pressed its threading into my skin and the doctor had to cut into me to remove the bits of gauze. The nurse gave me a number of shots for the pain. Then the surgeon, using tweezers, started to withdraw the rods. Each squeaked as it was loosened and withdrawn from my flesh.

With splints to apply at night, an introduction to a physical therapist, and strict orders to take good care of myself, I was discharged. In the meantime, with the money given to her by Uncle Abdulkadir, Sahra enrolled in a private school to qualify as a secretary with foreign language skills. Everyone expected that I would look after Rashid and Madame La Lune and take care of the housework. When I asked how soon I'd be able to continue my schooling, Sahra answered that there was no money for me.

In the spring they operated on my left hand. This time when I woke from the anesthesia I could no longer feel my middle finger. At first, the doctors assured me that it was an effect of the painkiller. But several days later the finger was still numb, so I was operated on for the third time. Still, the finger remained stiff. It had assumed an untoward twenty-degree angle. Nobody admitted that a mistake had been made. Instead, they started planning to operate on my feet. "The toes, too, should be straightened," they said. Each time weeks passed before the metal rods were removed. Each time I screamed when I heard the metal squeaking in my flesh. After the fifth operation nine fingers and a pair of toes were nearly straight, one finger had lost all feeling, and my big toe was now more crooked than ever. I was forced to walk on the outsides of my feet.

In the meantime, Sahra had given birth. While she was in school, I took care of little Mursel as well as Rashid and Madame La Lune, whose dementia was increasing. It was a challenge but one that gave me pride. From time to time, when Mursel had a fever or cried because he was teething, I would miss my physical therapy. At night I sometimes forgot to put on the splints because it was best if the baby, whom I now loved above all else, fell asleep on my stomach. Half a year after having been discharged from the clinic, my fingers started to become crooked again. I ignored them.

Back in Mogadishu, Aunt Madeleine and Uncle Abdulkadir had divorced. For years, Aunt Madeleine's family had been ashamed of their unorthodox son-in-law. Now that nobody's feelings had to be spared, the rage they had long nourished burst out. Sahra, her mother, who had arrived recently, and Madame La Lune criticized Uncle Abdulkadir. They complained also about Aunt Madeleine, who had been stupid to marry him in the first place. And they criticized me because I was Uncle Abdulkadir's niece, a member of that unholy clan that had made Aunt Madeleine so unhappy. The women now looked me over scornfully, directing their gaze toward my hands, dropping their eyes to my feet, and calling me a pitiful cripple.

I took refuge in the broom closet and locked myself in. I longed for Aunt Madeleine, whom I loved, just as I loved Uncle Abdulkadir. My inability to help either of them tortured me. And I missed my mother and my sister. I asked Sahra for permission to phone Mogadishu, but it became too complicated. I would have to register my call and then wait around for hours for a connection. It was also expensive. At night I lay awake for hours, my body like lead and my heart heavy. At some point, I would close my eyes and imagine myself standing in a palace, in a foyer full of light and flowers, with white curtains puffed by gentle breezes at open windows, with birds singing, and on the terrace I would hear Uncle Abdulkadir and Aunt Madeleine receiving guests. Glasses would clink, music would sound, and soon I would go out there to be pleasantly greeted, to make my own compliments, to enjoy compliments from others admiring my petal-white dress and my new pumps. And the ambassadors of foreign lands would kiss my stunningly beautiful hands.

Ibrahim was unable to find work, so he and Sahra decided, after a year and a half in Munich, to try their luck in the United Arab Emirates. The movers marched in and out, packing crates. "What will you do?" Sahra asked as she spied me, shortly before they left, taking my few possessions out of the last remaining wardrobe.

"I'm packing."

"Did you really think we were going to take you with us?"

I turned to dust.

The day they were to fly, the movers picked up the last boxes. Voices echoed against the naked walls. With Mursel on my arm, I stood at the window and looked down at the street. The furniture truck glistened blue in the sun. Nobody saw me.

"Where should I go?" I asked.

Sahra was combing her hair. "Call your uncle," she replied without looking up. "Maybe he'll help you." Mursel passed a bit of paper over my cheek. I made believe it tickled, and that got him laughing. The thought that in a moment I would have to hand him over forever caused me severe pain. I felt hollowed out.

"Do you remember the people in Augsburg who visited us a few weeks ago?" Sahra asked. "The Somali with the German husband and the little child? Maybe you can live with them."

"But I saw her only once. I don't know her!"

"It would only be for a couple of months. Until they can send you a plane ticket."

"But . . ."

"Do you have any better idea?"

"Maybe they don't want anyone else living with them."

"I'll phone her . . ." The shrill of the horn cut Sahra short. Below, next to the furniture truck, stood a taxi. Madame La Lune put on her coat and swayed as she reached for her hat. Sahra approached me and took Mursel.

Time stood still.

I heard the door close.

I don't know how long I sat there.

At some point, I remember, a cry rose in my chest—an immense pressure grew and then broke, shattering the stillness. Its echo fell back from the walls and pierced my breast, crashing into my body. I felt as though a club had been pounding my torso. At the same time, I wanted someone to hit me—anything so that I might feel again.

Where could I go?

Slowly, I grew more tranquil. Then, as a key turned in the front door lock, Jamal came in. He had not left with the others. "Come," he said, still standing on the threshold and observing me. "I'm driving you to Augsburg."

Yes, then I remembered. They had come once to visit and stayed the whole afternoon—Waris, a Somali, Detlef, her German husband, and Saïd, their son. Now she stood before me and said, "Welcome!" and as I hesitated to mount the step, "I've made us some tea."

I had been sweating, freezing, and in a frenzy, considering my options. What would I do if this woman didn't want me? Then Waris took my suitcase, placed it next to the wardrobe, and pushed me gently into the living room. On the table was a cake, on the couch, Saïd. He was pouting. But suddenly, his mouth pulled itself into a big smile. He recognized me and laughed, and I hugged him and gave him a kiss.

"Please take a seat," Detlef said and pointed to an armchair.

"Are you going to be my big sister now?" asked Saïd. I touched his cheek with mine. He had already asked me that in Munich while I played with him and Mursel as the adults talked. So there we sat in the living room, drinking tea and eating cake. Gradually the fear drained out of my body. In the evening we cooked a Somali dish together. Detlef and Waris helped me make my bed. That night I dreamed of Mursel.

Whenever I jumped up to help with the housework, Detlef told me to sit down again. He gave me books and forbade me to act like a servant. We cooked and washed up together, played games or watched TV. Waris and Detlef registered me in a language school, helped me to find babysitting jobs and to extend my visa. They saw to it that I had health insurance, and they invested the money that Uncle Abdulkadir sent. They also phoned him in Mogadishu.

"Fadumo," said Uncle Abdulkadir in a voice riddled with exhaustion, "stay in Germany. Don't come back. There's no future here."

And once again I felt rejected.

I held on that much more to Waris, Detlef, and Saïd.

Waris took me along when she visited friends. Detlef's mother, Grandma Paula, whom everyone called *Ayeeyo*—Somali for grandmother—took me to the movies. Detlef's father, whom the family called *Ami*, for uncle, gave me money for an iced coffee. "Go out, Fadumo," Detlef said. "Go and meet other young people."

"Go out dancing," Waris said. "Live!"

When they moved elsewhere in Augsburg, they took me with them.

Outside it was raining—thick drops exploded on the windowpanes. On the table there were roasted lamb and other dishes. "Help yourself," my new friend Maryan said. I dipped the spoon into the curried rice and rejoiced at the smell. "I'm so glad you made it," said Udo, Maryan's German boyfriend. I forked a raisin and put it into my mouth. The radio was playing James Brown. "After eating we'll go to the Olympic Stadium. There's a fantastic Mardi Gras party."

"Hm," Maryan answered. "What should I put on?"

"It's already pretty late," I objected. We had started cooking at eight o'clock and it was now ten-thirty. The last train from Munich to Augsburg left at midnight. I knew I could spend the night at Maryan's, however, since I had done so before. She was a friend of Waris, a Somali trying to make a career as a model in Munich.

"Well, I could go as an African woman," Maryan grinned, stuffing a forkful of vegetables into her mouth.

"Not a bad idea," Udo replied. "You'd probably be the only one there who didn't need makeup."

"But I don't have a costume," I said. On the radio, Aretha Franklin replaced James Brown.

"We'll find something," Maryan said and shoved her plate aside. "Come on," she added, pulling me behind her. "Let's explore the closet."

Shortly before midnight two African princesses in glittering veils, escorted by a pirate in jeans and hiking boots, could be seen waiting for the tram.

The building was full. Udo, Maryan, and I stood squashed together next to the entrance, and for a moment I lost all desire to squeeze in. But I quickly adjusted my veil, hooked my arm into Maryan's, and competing with the music, shouted, "Okay! Let's celebrate!" Udo performed a long, drawn-out whistle. "Let's go!"

We snaked through gigolos and transvestites, a mountain of a mushroom blocking the way, and Captain Ahab flirting with an Eskimo girl. A doctor with a surgical mask raised his stein to Udo, bellowing, "Cheers!" Next to the doctor stood Frankenstein with huge plastic hands, facial scars, a full beard, and hair to his hips. "Should I find you a table?" Frankenstein offered, grinning.

I grinned back. "Of course! And fast—" Frankenstein vanished into the crowd, but to my surprise, a few moments later, he reappeared with coffee and jelly donuts. "Come with me," he said and gestured toward a corner. We tagged along.

Frankenstein really had found a table. "What's your name?" he asked once we'd sat down. He offered me a cup of coffee. I took it with my hands angled so he couldn't see my fingers.

"Fatima," I answered. That was the name most Germans assigned to me since Fadumo was too difficult for them to pronounce.

"I'm Walter." I drank to him using my coffee mug, lifted my veil, and bit the jelly donut. The marmalade oozed out the sides.

"Are you from the Maldives?"

"From Somalia."

"Amazing. I have a friend from the Maldives, also called Fatima. And you could be twins."

"Of course," I said, asking myself why he was telling me this. Maryan and Udo got up to dance. "Would you like to?" Frankenstein asked. I hesitated. The deejay was playing Nina Simone, and I had to think about how you danced to this sort of music. I nodded, and Frankenstein held out his gigantic hand.

At about 3 a.m., when we were all exhausted, he offered to drive us home. The subway had stopped running, so we accepted with pleasure. The Beetle stopped in front of Maryan's house. We got out, said good-bye, and the car rattled away.

A couple of days later the bell rang. At the door of Waris's and Detlef's house stood Frankenstein, this time minus the scars and plastic hands, though his hair continued to reach his hips. A hippie, I thought. What would Waris and Detlef say? For an instant I searched for words. "Hello," he said.

"How . . . How did you find my address?" I asked.

"I asked Maryan." Under his beard I saw a grin. "But I had to beg for a long time."

"Who's there?" Waris called from the hallway. "Oh," she said, "a guest. Come in!" Saïd was rumbling around in the living room. Hesitantly, I stepped aside and Walter entered.

Waris offered coffee and cake. Detlef shook his hand, and minutes later the men stood out on the balcony, talking. Two hours later they were still talking, and I was getting increasingly nervous. "What were you chatting about for so long?" I hissed when Detlef came in to go to the bathroom.

"About this and that."

"What does that mean? Give me a real answer," I nagged. "Please . . ."

Detlef merely looked at me. "Really. He's okay." Then he closed the bathroom door.

Walter impressed me with his travel stories. Only a few days before the Mardi Gras party, he had returned from a trip around the world. As a photographer he had been to Iran, Turkey, Sri Lanka, and India, and he'd crossed deserts. When he ran out of money, he had worked as a cook, a hotel manager, or in any job he could find. In Australia he was in construction. For a while he had tended lepers in a hospice run by Mother Teresa. In the Maldives he had fallen ill with malaria. That was something I could talk about, too, so, laughing, we compared symptoms: shivering followed by fever succeeded by freezing. Walter saw the world through a camera lens. He was interested not only in the beauty of nature but in people's daily lives. He wanted to know how they lived and he wanted to preserve his impressions. He taught me things about countries I had never heard of and, not coincidentally, my German improved remarkably. Waris, Detlef, Saïd, Ami, and Ayeeyo also liked Walter. That made me happy.

The first time I spent the night at Walter's, he said, "I know you're Muslim, and what that means. You don't have any reason to be afraid of me." He put new sheets on the bed and puffed up the pillow. "You'll sleep here and I'll take the couch."

The next morning as we entered the kitchen, Walter's mother gave a start. The brush with which she had been cleaning a dish nearly fell from her hand. "Good morning," Walter said. After his return he had moved back into his parents' house while looking for a place of his own. Taking two mugs from the cupboard, he asked, "Would you like a cup of coffee, Fatima?"

114

Walter's father sat at the table, his head bent over a newspaper. The room drowned in silence broken only by the ticking clock. I could hardly bring myself to nod.

"You bringin' the likes of her around here?" Although I didn't understand her Bavarian accent at first, it was clear she would prefer I go to hell. But why? What had I done to her?

"Mother!" Walter said, his voice sharp as steel. I'd never heard it like that before. "Fatima's my girlfriend, and she can visit whenever she wants to."

"Your girlfriend?" She spit the words on the floor, directly in front of my feet. Slowly, her stare traced my body from head to toe; her eyes stopped at my hands. I shivered. "What's up with her hands? Just take a look at those mitts!"

"Mother." Crash went the coffee cup. His father peered for a second over the top of his paper before sinking into it again, silent, as if he weren't really there. Walter's mother stiffened her shoulders, straightened her apron, and stepped back. Leaning against the stove, arms folded over her chest, she fixed me with her gaze. "Don't think for a minute that you'll get him. He deserves better," she hissed. Walter pushed me quickly from the kitchen. In his room he threw a pair of pants and a couple of shirts into a suitcase, packed his camera equipment, and grabbed his keys.

That summer Walter and I moved into a small apartment. We got along very well, talking, laughing, taking short trips. We were in love and knew we wanted to spend the rest of our lives together. My family didn't know that, unmarried, I was living with a man, but I feared they might hear about me, and, indeed, the idea itself worried me.

One day in March, under a clear sky, with the Alps in the distance, I awoke, my head hurting. The evening before we'd attended a concert and had been out late. I put on my slippers. Walter was still asleep; in half an hour I'd wake him up.

In the kitchen I put bread into the toaster and some water on the stove. From the refrigerator, I poured two glasses of orange juice. I soft-boiled eggs and placed them, marmalade, honey, bread, butter, and tea on a tray, and carried it into the bedroom. Walter stretched. I plucked at his beard and balanced the tray next to the bed. "Do you think your parents will come?"

"I don't know. But it doesn't matter."

"Of course it matters." I slipped under the covers.

"If my mother wants things to be like this, it's her decision." Walter decapitated his egg. "We can't do anything about it." I sighed. After Walter had told his parents that we were getting married, his mother had been furious. For weeks they had fought. Finally, Walter threatened them: Not only would we marry, but he'd take my name. That made me feel almost sorry for his mother. She scolded and insulted me, but still, was it right to treat your parents like that? Children turning away from their parents was unthinkable in Somalia. The idea alone made me ill. But, two days before, my future mother-in-law had announced that she was considering the matter and might come to the wedding after all. I really hoped she would. I longed for family, peace, and harmony.

During the car trip home the night before the wedding, a high-pitched sound invaded my ear, and I had to turn up the radio to understand what was being said. "I'm still half deaf from the concert."

"The main thing is that you hear the prompt when you're supposed to say 'yes,'" Walter grinned.

"Could you maybe give me a sign?"

Walter's godmother was already waiting for us outside city hall. His friends, Sonja and Ernst, were also there, standing to one side and waving. Many of his friends still met me with reserve; only Sonja had wholeheartedly embraced me. For that reason I had asked her to be my witness. Waris and Detlef couldn't be there because they were away, as were Maryan and Udo. Walter found a parking space, signaled, and backed in. A woman's shriek sounded from in front of city hall. Walter stomped on the brakes. Out of the car's blind spot his father appeared with his mother in tow.

Walter had nearly run them over.

The civil ceremony was to take place in an unadorned room. Walter's mother strode directly toward a seat in the first row. She pressed her handbag to her chest and was uncharacteristically quiet. Sonja chattered all the more, pulled at my dress and my hair, carried my bouquet. She was clearly more nervous than I was. Walter greeted a colleague who had agreed to take photos. For the wedding, my future husband had cut off his hip-length hair. I still wasn't used to the way he looked. Walter's father adjusted his tie and then seated himself next to his wife. As always, he was silent and seemed to not really belong.

I looked around.

On a table next to the justice of the peace were two candles. The few guests seemed lost in the big room. For a moment I remembered the extravagant weddings in my country—the intoxicating celebrations for which parents saved for years so that for days they could fete hundreds of guests who brought many gifts. The thought made me sad. Eva, Walter's only sister and my future sister-in-law, was also absent. Walter and Eva got along, but their mother wasn't fond of her own daughter. In any case, I thought, it suits my life to marry into a family that feuds. I was used to that.

A hand found its way between Walter and me. I stepped aside. Walter's mother hugged her son, held him tight, and, crying, wished him future happiness. Then, abruptly, she let him go, stepped back, and tripped, falling against a vase in which Sonja had put the bouquet. The vase fell, knocking over a candle that ignited the flowers. My bouquet went up in flames.

I nearly cried.

Outside the sky streamed the most beautiful blue.

To be married meant to have children and that meant I had to be opened. But how would I manage that? What could I do? No one had ever talked to me about these things. I missed my mother, Khadija, my cousin Nadifo—the women in the family who could help a woman do what had to be done.

For months Walter and I were chaste and embarrassed with

each other, each thinking about how to broach the topic. We were young: I was nineteen, and Walter was twenty-four. We laughed and fooled around, but we had no words for the unspeakable. From time to time we gave each other a little kiss. And it could have continued like that. Because none of Walter's friends could lend us a car, and we didn't want to ask his parents for their help, we used the tram to move our things to a larger apartment. We felt strong, even invincible; difficulties bound us together.

But the feeling that I was missing a part of marriage never let me go; it grew and grew, ever more powerful. I also felt guilty and responsible. One day I said timidly, "I'm going to see a doctor."

My suggestion took Walter's breath away.

The office occupied the fourth floor of a pre–World War I apartment house. The entry smelled of cleanser that had just been applied to the still-moist stairs. Someone had been mopping. Nevertheless, the place was shabby.

Next to the door was a sign. I rang, and the door was buzzed open. A mature woman in large gold earrings and red lipstick peered at me over the tops of her glasses. "What can I do for you?"

"I have an appointment with the doctor." I gave my name and put my insurance card on the counter.

"Take a seat, please."

In the waiting room other women were seated, none, one glance told me, younger than fifty. I greeted them, but most didn't look up. I took a newspaper, sat down, and thumbed through it, but could not concentrate enough to read. My throat was completely dry. I swallowed, but a lump simply wouldn't go down.

I had no idea what might be done to me.

Every time the assistant came in holding a card and calling out a name, her earrings clanged. Her feet were slipped into robust, supportive shoes with open backs that looked professional but clashed with her more dressy clothing.

"Mrs. . . ." She glanced at the card in her hand. "Koro?"

"Cracow," a woman said, rising.

"No, Koro," the assistant corrected. "Is anybody here named Koro?" She looked around, her glance stopping at me. "That must be you, such an African sound . . ."

"The name is Korn. Fadumo Korn."

"Right, that's what I said." From her pocket she extracted a pen. "Nobody can read this scribble. Come with me." In silence I followed.

She opened a door. A screen divided the room. To the right stood a desk. "The doctor will be with you shortly," she said, gesturing toward a chair.

The door closed.

Silence. No voices. Not a sound could be heard.

I sat down on the chair. On the wall behind the desk were metal cabinets, and behind glass doors boxes of medicines were piled high. On a ledge stood a cactus, joined on the windowsill by two smaller ones, its offshoots. My hands were ice cold.

As the door opened, I jumped. An old man entered. Swiftly, the notion shot through my head that the doctor, his helper, and the cacti had all suddenly aged. Soon spiderwebs would have covered them. He sat down on the other side of the desk, glanced at my record and health insurance card, requested my name, address, and date of birth. "What's the problem?" he asked. Blood rushed to my head, and my heart beat so loudly I was sure it would drown out my voice. The doctor looked at me. I opened my mouth. Closed it. Opened it.

"I'd like you to examine me."

"Then get undressed. I'll be right back." With his right hand he gestured toward the screen while with the left he patted the earth under his cacti and shook his head. "Mrs. Gruber," he called, disappearing through the door. I got up, approached the screen, and froze.

I wanted to turn around and flee.

"Are you ready?" The doctor returned, a watering can in his hand. I darted behind the divider. With stiff fingers I unzipped my jeans—plunging into an infinite shame—yet I forced myself to carry out what I had come there to do. Water splashed, meeting dry earth. In a T-shirt that reached almost to my knees, I stepped out. "Please," said the doctor, putting on rubber gloves, gesturing toward the examining table. I was incapable of movement, shaking, freezing, defenseless. I felt vulnerably naked and exposed. I whispered Khadija's name to myself. She would have known what to do.

"You have to take off *all* your clothes." A hand pushed me toward the chair. I wanted to scream and do something really bad, anything just to get away, to escape. "Place your legs in these stirrups." His hand grasped a lamp over his head and pulled it down. I obeyed. Closed my eyes. Made as if it were not me lying there.

A shriek.

"My god!" The doctor's head shot up, colliding with the lamp. "Child, what have they done to you?" he screeched. The door flew open. The assistant came in.

"Doctor?"

The physician struggled for air. I heard his chair rolling over the floor, heard footsteps. "I'm sorry. There's nothing I can do for you. You'll have to see another doctor."

The door shut. Silence.

I cried as I hadn't since my mother died. I felt dirty, rejected. A doctor, an educated professional whose job it was to examine women, had run screaming from the sight of me. No other woman had fled his office sobbing. They had all appeared happy, relieved. What was so monstrous about me? Was there some awful growth between my legs, something I hadn't noticed that made me untouchable?

I crept into bed. Walter tried to comfort me, but I was inconsolable. I wanted to die. Only when Maryan phoned did I tell her what had happened. "Good grief," she exclaimed. "You ended up with an old fart who doesn't know his ass from his elbow." For a moment I was angry to hear her disrespectful tone. "I know a good doctor," she said firmly. "I'll make an appointment for you."

"No! Never! I'm never going to see a doctor again."

"So what will you do with your husband?"

I kept quiet.

"Fadumo, in Africa older people are considered wise and experienced, and therefore they are respected. In Germany it's sometimes exactly the opposite. Often younger doctors have been better educated and are more sensitive to their patients' problems. I'll go with you to a doctor who knows about female circumcision."

"Do you mean I have a problem because I'm circumcised?"

Now Maryan was silent. After a while she said, "Yes, Fadumo."

"But . . ." My head spun. I remembered Saïda and Aunt Madeleine—but Aunt Madeleine was an extraordinary person. "I mean," I said, "so . . . German women aren't circumcised?"

"No, Fadumo."

"But . . . but that's disgusting!" I swallowed. Actually, I almost laughed. It sounded so absurd. "You mean, all the women in this country are dirty?"

"Well, they're not circumcised." A spontaneous feeling of superiority came over me—just a hint at first, then my pride grew. It filled me up, carried me, and erased my shame, shoving sadness aside. I was clean in a country of the unclean.

A child chosen by God.

Maryan came to my house. We took the subway to the doctor's office in a postwar building. The rooms were bright and friendly with pictures of desert safaris and innumerable newborns on the walls. There were no cacti or older assistants. Nonetheless, I was shaking. "He is really nice," Maryan assured me, pressing my hand. "And believe me, he's a good doctor."

A blond, not very large man entered the waiting room. He had a mustache and offered me both his hands, as we did at home if we wanted to show someone special respect. "A new patient," he said. "Hello."

I greeted him in return. Why was he beaming at me like that?

"Please." Dr. Schmidt gestured toward a leather chair and pulled his seat up alongside it. Stiffly I sat there, my eyes directed at the

121

gynecologist, waiting for a single, shaming sentence: Please undress. "Don't worry," Dr. Schmidt said. "I'm not going to examine you."

"No?" It was almost too good to believe.

"No," Dr. Schmidt smiled. "I know why you're here. I suggest we do this: My assistant will arrange an appointment at the hospital. There I'll operate. You won't feel a thing because you get . . . " He smiled more broadly. "I call it the 'blue dream.'"

"What's a 'blue dream'?"

"A narcotic." He talked as if something fine awaited me, something to be happy about. His voice was convincing, even if I didn't understand what the operation was meant to do.

"I'm aware that women in your country are infibulated. In order to have intercourse and become pregnant they have to be opened." In an instant my euphoria vanished. I heard the word "opened."

"I assure you, you won't feel a thing," said Dr. Schmidt. "After the operation you'll have pain, but you'll also receive medication to stop it."

My back hurt again. And again an icy cold crept up my spine.

In Somalia a woman is opened on her wedding night. Sometimes she does it herself, with a knife; sometimes an aunt, the mother-in-law, or the husband does it.

Sometimes the wound closes up again. Some women give birth without ever having been really opened. In that case, the scar tissue around the vagina can't stretch, and they can bleed to death or the baby can be smothered. Thus the long-term side effects of infibulation can be lethal for mother and child. Yet, some men insist that, after giving birth, their wives be sewn up again.

In the hospital, reversing infibulation takes about half an hour. But complications can occur: The surgeon might discover a football-sized cyst, wild growths, strange scarring, dead leaves of flesh that had been blocking the minute opening for years. Often, surgeons have to treat old wounds of the urethra, vagina, anus, and perineum.

Walter went with me to the clinic. Hugging me good-bye, he said, "Everything's going to be all right. Don't be afraid."

I wasn't afraid. I was panicked.

In the bed next to mine a young woman was crying. She had just lost her baby. I wept and wished that no one would touch me ever again. Softly I crept under the sheet and wrapped myself up in it, further and tighter, until I lay like a mummy in the white bed. When I closed my eyes, I saw the clearing. Sometimes I heard the squeaking of a thorn. My circumcision was thousands of miles away, and yet I remained fearful of the excisor's dirty fingers and the pain they had wrought.

The night before the operation I couldn't keep my legs still. The fidgeting began in my heels and migrated to my belly. I ran to the toilet, convinced I was getting a bladder infection. At some point I asked the night nurse for a sleeping pill.

In the morning a male nurse wheeled me into the operating room—cold light, naked tiles, voices echoing from the walls, hurried steps, somewhere, a scream. A doctor—I didn't know him—leaned over me and felt my pulse. I was shaking, my teeth chattering with fear. My whole body heaved. Suddenly I saw Dr. Schmidt, felt his smile and warm hand on my cheek. An anesthesiologist said, "I gave her a double dose." My body resisted. A mask covered my face. There were noises, clanking, as if the world were clattering into a pail. Colors disappeared, replaced by a white fog that crept into my limbs—wet and cold. My body heaved once more—I felt it only from a distance.

Then everything went white.

I woke up sobbing like a baby because I didn't know where I was or what had happened. Completely overwhelmed, I lay there, my cheeks wet, the pillow moist. I couldn't stop the tears. A nurse took me in her arms, murmured some words I didn't understand, and stroked my head. At some point I fell asleep again.

The next day Maryan and Walter visited, and, in the afternoon, Dr. Schmidt came. "You're quite a patient," he said, pulling a chair up to the bedside. "You really kept us busy."

"Was I cracking bad jokes?"

"No, you were stalking lions and hunting hyenas. You were

123

somewhere in the steppe, defending yourself with arms and legs. We almost had to tie you down."

"Sorry." My stomach hurt, but I could smile again.

"So how are you?" Dr. Schmidt asked.

"My body feels dull, gray somehow."

"We've given you painkillers. The operation took a long time, nearly three hours. Luckily I found no cysts, only blood that had never been expelled." Dr. Schmidt thumbed his mustache. "If I may say so, the excisor did a pretty thorough job. I had to improvise a little." Sometimes brutality can only be described ironically. "But you'll see. In a few weeks you'll be jumping around like a deer."

In the meantime, I crept through the corridors like a grandmother. Often enough I had to be carried. When I was in bed, the nurses turned me from the left to the right side, just as my mother had once done. Every movement of my legs, every leaning and bending hurt. And always, the real pain confused itself with the remembered one from twelve years before. More than anything else, I was afraid of going to the bathroom. I couldn't produce a drop, and this time it wasn't because the opening was too small. It was remembering how the sting of the urine felt running over an open wound. Doctors encouraged me, assured me that my blood contained so high a dose of painkillers that it was physically impossible for me to suffer. But memory was powerful. Again, I stopped drinking. Again, I cursed my lower body and wanted to get rid of it, to leave it behind, and never deal with it ever, ever again.

One week after the operation, I was discharged.

When alone, I slithered on my stomach through the apartment. Otherwise Walter took care of me. Because Dr. Schmidt had prescribed medicinal baths, twice a day Walter lifted me into the bathtub, and fifteen minutes later he heaved me out. My husband helped me when I had to use the toilet. He assured me that he was glad to be of use. But I felt ashamed. Six weeks later the wounds had healed.

During this time, my life changed.

Never had I imagined it could be so easy to empty my bladder. What a powerful stream! What a feeling of relief after only a few seconds! Till now I'd spent ten, twenty, even thirty minutes on the toilet, pressing and squeezing. I used to drink very little, which led to painful kidneys. But how could I have explained to an employer why it took me half an hour to go to the bathroom?

Now it was almost a pleasure to go.

Even greater was my surprise one morning to discover a spot of blood on the sheet. I was a little afraid that the wound had opened, but it was my period. No ripping, no rumbling. My stomach didn't hurt, I had no cramps, I didn't even have to throw up, and after only four days, it was over. I felt light and laughed, felt a tickling behind my belly button and laughed more loudly. I breathed in and breathed out, and felt for the first time since that morning in the clearing that air could stream deep inside my body. I felt cheerful and free.

In the coming months as well, my periods came and went without incident. The panic that had become habitual at their approach gradually diminished. No longer was I compelled to change jobs every couple of months because, during menstruation, I would be absent for several days. I began to use makeup, to change my hair style, and to take care of myself.

From time to time I discovered evidence of a discharge. I changed my underpants, washed, and douched. "You're destroying the vaginal flora," Dr. Schmidt said. "You'll get infections." I got infections. But I was unable to stop washing. The discharge was uncomfortable. It made me feel as dirty as a drooling child. "The discharge is perfectly normal," Dr. Schmidt said. But this normality was foreign to me. It took awhile to get used to it.

Most stubborn, however, was fear of the unspeakable.

In Walter I had an intimate friend to whom I felt bound by much that had happened to us. We loved each other, and I would have been perfectly content for the relationship to remain platonic. I would have liked Dr. Schmidt to inseminate me. I wanted an adult version of the childhood play with Nadifo: squatting, sneezing, and birthing the baby with ease.

"I can't sleep with a man," I said.

"Yes, you can," Dr. Schmidt replied.

Whenever I visited his office, Walter came with me. Dr. Schmidt took time to talk to us about sex. He counseled Walter, telling him to be considerate. He also told Walter not to pressure me—which he had never done in any case. He informed us that during the operation he had removed a lot of dead flesh, that my skin would still be numb, but, with time, I'd begin to feel something. He said, "You both need to develop your fantasies." He often talked in the plural, or about "us three," as if we were a team working on a common project. "Lust and sensitivity can be learned," he said. But really, I didn't want to feel. My experience had taught me that touching my body meant only torture.

"Discover your body," Dr. Schmidt repeated again and again. "Touch yourself—with your fingers, with a feather. Find out what satisfies you." I stared at him, completely at sea, and sometimes shipwrecked.

"Never!" I swore. Allah would kill me. Lightning would strike. Maybe I'd be sterile! I wanted at least five children.

"Sex takes place in your head, not between your legs," Dr. Schmidt said. "Enjoy your body."

"Leave me alone," I responded harshly more than once.

Two years after the wedding we had the honeymoon.

7

A man stood at the door. He was wearing a gray suit, a tie, and a light trench coat. He smiled politely and said, "Good day. I'm from the city of Munich." Then he gave me his name.

A representative of the German government in our apartment—I was surprised but, of course, let him in. "Would you like a cup of tea?" I asked, pushing a couple of newspapers aside to clear the table. "Please, sit down." I took his coat. The man opened a few buttons on his jacket. I put the water on to boil and asked, "What can I do for you?"

"Well," he said, searching for documents in his briefcase. "We have a few open questions."

Walter came out of the bathroom, and I introduced our guest.

"A very nice apartment you have here," the gentleman said, looking around as I put tea in the teapot.

"Yes, we were lucky," I answered. "But we had to do a lot of renovating."

"Two rooms?"

"Yes, and a small balcony." I placed the cups on the table with a plate of cookies and poured the tea. The gentleman took a sip. When he put the cup down, it splattered, and he apologized.

"No problem," I said, jumping up and grabbing a towel.

"Can I use the toilet?"

"Of course." I dried my hands. "The first door on the left. Wait a minute. I'll show you."

"Thank you, but don't go to any trouble."

In the bedroom, Walter was shaking out the bedclothes.

"That's an unusually large bedroom," the gentleman said returning from the bathroom. "Very nice, really, very nice."

"Take a look around," Walter said, not very politely.

The gentleman finished his tea. Shortly thereafter he put his documents back in the briefcase. "Well, I won't disturb you any longer," he said. "In case any further questions arise, I'll be back in touch."

"Of course, any time," I said, wondering what this was all about. He hadn't asked me anything. I accompanied him to the door.

"Do you know what that was?" Walter queried as I put the empty teacup in the dishwasher.

"A representative of the German government," I said.

"A spy who was trying to find out if we had married only so you could get a residency permit!"

The idea wasn't entirely new to me. Before our wedding, a woman working for the government had asked Walter how much I had paid him to marry me. The suspicion had enraged me. Later a bureaucrat had said we couldn't marry because I couldn't produce a birth certificate. In tears I had run to the Somali consulate, only a few blocks away, to find a friend of my uncle. Storming into a meeting I had thrown myself into his arms. "Girl," he had exclaimed. "What have they done to you?" Five days later we had gained permission to marry.

The court clerk had forced me to take Walter's name, a requirement I resented, for in Somalia it would have been cause for revenge. We give a child a name of its own and then add the names of father and grandfather to identify the heritage. Altering one's name betrays the family. I had refused, but without success. So bureaucracy changed Fadumo Abdi Hersi Farah Husen to Faduma Korn. "Fadumo isn't a woman's name," the official had explained to me.

128

"But I am a woman," I had retorted.

"Here no woman's name ends in 'o.'"

When I had left the office, I was Faduma, and as if that wasn't humiliating enough, they had made me sign the documents that changed my name. Then, to extend my visa, which, since the wedding I had had to do once a year, I had to run an obstacle course. And after all of that, a permanent residence permit would be granted only after five years of marriage.

We had a beautiful apartment. I had women friends—something I'd never experienced before, since it's difficult for a nomad to give friendships the time they deserve. Even in Mogadishu, I had lived mainly within the family. Walter worked as a press photographer for a newspaper. After having cared for babies, washed dishes, and clerked in shops, I was employed in a bookbindery. The work was difficult, and sometimes my hands hurt, but it was fun to restore old books. On holidays we traveled to Greece and Algeria, to Malaysia, Thailand, and Hong Kong. I would have liked children right away, but when Walter suggested waiting a few years, I agreed. I was happy to know I belonged somewhere. For so long I had moved aimlessly, alone and unloved. From my siblings, I received long letters. We also recorded tapes for each other and, from time to time, I phoned Uncle Abdulkadir.

We enjoyed life in Munich.

In Somalia, where I could have returned at any time, my family would have provided a house for us. We could have had servants. My husband could have worked in one of my uncle's companies or created a firm of his own. We could have lived very comfortably among Mogadishu's elite.

Either way, the world seemed to be ours.

The connection hissed, interrupted from time to time by a woman's voice. Just as I was about to hang up, Uncle Abdulkadir took the receiver. I held my breath and said, "Uncle, I've gotten married."

Dead silence. Only static and the woman speaking.

"I'll call you back," Uncle Abdulkadir said. Then the dial tone. I waited an hour, pacing nervously back and forth in the apartment. I was afraid. Had I not kept it secret, my family would have forbidden the marriage. "You've gotten married," my uncle said, after the telephone finally rang. "So there's nothing to be done about it?"

"No, Uncle."

"Is he Somali?"

"No. German."

"At least you didn't marry a nigger." For a moment I was speechless. In Germany I was the one called a nigger. But Somalis, too, were racist. Because they were relatively light-skinned, they assumed they were superior to darker-skinned Africans. Marriage to a black African—in my family's eyes—would have been a union unequal to my status.

Three years after our wedding Khadija began to nag about wanting to meet my husband. I would rather have waited until we had our first child, but it really was time for Walter to get to know my family. So we decided to fly to Somalia. To Walter, I had been a young girl without artifice or arrogance until I started to tell him about my family. I talked of villas and power, about one uncle who headed the secret service, another who was Minister of Finance, and a third who controlled the government printing office. I told him about my brother, who had participated in liberating hostages from the Lufthansa plane skyjacked in 1977, and mentioned my uncle, the president. At times my husband looked at me as if I were some exotic bird; at others, as if he didn't believe a word. Sometimes he simply lost count of the relatives.

All these relatives would be expecting presents—expensive offerings to mollify them because our union had already been consummated. Especially important were the gifts for my father. They constituted the bride-price. Walter had to make up for not having asked formally for my hand. My father sent a cassette. As I thrust it into the machine and his voice came on, for a moment I was again his little girl. Slowly, always looking for just the right word, my

130

father spoke: First, he gave thanks to Allah, then to the spirits, then to his children and parents-in-law, until finally, he named his gifts: an aluminum trunk and a radio. My brother Muhammad, who in the meantime had become a successful tennis player, wanted a racket, gym shoes, socks, and tennis balls. Khadija asked for perfume. Uncle Abdulkadir didn't want a present, but I bought him a bottle of his favorite Christian Dior cologne. And we purchased toys for the children.

With a considerable number of large suitcases, we flew from Munich to Rome to Mogadishu. Shortly before landing, the flight attendant distributed forms. "You don't have to make a financial declaration," I said.

"Why not?" Walter asked.

"Because we aren't going to go through either passport control or customs." My husband looked at me quizzically and insisted on declaring his funds.

On the runway a black limousine was already waiting.

Uncle Abdulkadir had moved. His new house was easily more grand than that of the evicted Russian ambassador. On our first afternoon he held a reception, and the entire family poured in to stare at Fadumo and her white husband. Walter and I, after more than thirty hours of traveling, had to shake innumerable hands. In the evening—it was December 31—the reception blurred into a New Year's party, and we were called upon to join the celebration. When the older people withdrew for a more formal dinner, Uncle Abdulkadir seemed displeased, but he said nothing.

My cousins, all of whom spoke English, drowned Walter in questions about his life in Germany. Shortly before midnight, as we climbed up onto the roof, four of my cousins placed themselves squarely on the stairs, raised their right arms, snapped their heels together, and shouted, "*Heil* Hitler!"

Walter paled.

"Why are they doing that?" he whispered, shocked.

"Because they want to give you the warmest of welcomes."

My cousin asked, "Why isn't your husband happy? We practiced the whole day." One of them shook his head and said, "Everyone agrees it's courteous to welcome someone the way he's accustomed to being greeted back home."

I decided not to explain just then that "*Heil* Hitler" carried criminal sanctions in Germany, and that it was hardly possible to subject a former hippie to any worse greeting. Instead, I looked for a distraction. This was soon provided because in Somali celebrations we not only light fireworks but shoot live ammunition, too.

The following day another reception took place, then a banquet, visits, and more family celebrations. I saw my father again, now living not far from Mogadishu. I also saw Ahmed, who, after spending fifteen years in the army, had resigned because of a leg wound. He and his wife had eleven children. I met my father's third wife, who spread a cloth over the aluminum trunk and placed the new radio on top of it. A feeling of childhood affection for my father overwhelmed me when I saw how, despite having aged considerably, he stood with the same handsome dignity among his children and grandchildren, his red henna beard glistening in the sun. I hugged him. I hugged Jama and my little brother Muhammad. I asked Khadija for forgiveness since my marriage had broken a rule: Elder daughters must marry before younger ones. From a traditional point of view, violating this custom had insulted Khadija.

"It's a good thing you didn't wait," she told me, smiling. "I don't plan to marry. I love my brothers and want to live with them."

I knew that a number of men had already asked for her hand. Surprisingly, neither my father nor Uncle Abdulkadir had forced Khadija to accept them.

Khadija and the women in the family greeted Walter warmly. I valued the good opinion of my sister more than anyone else. She liked him. She stroked Walter's soft beard, his blond hair, and bubbled: "Like silk . . ."

"The important thing is, he's not Italian," my great aunt said.

Men reacted with greater reserve. My father talked to Walter as he did to nearly everyone else: timidly but politely. Some asked whether my husband had been circumcised, and whether he was a Muslim. "But of course," I answered. In fact, during a trip to the Maldives, Walter had converted. From then on the family called him Rashid.

In addition to many close relatives—including my uncle, cousins, and aunt—people I hardly remembered appeared and said, "You don't know me anymore?"

I lied. "Oh, yes, indeed!"

"I'm Aunt Masbal, cousin Leyla's second oldest sister."

I nodded. But who was Leyla?

"Where are the gifts for the family?"

"The shipment is on its way," I lied. The aunt looked me up and down before moving away, apparently satisfied with my response.

At the end of the second week, Walter refused to spend any more time at receptions. He wanted to see the countryside.

For days we fought with Uncle Abdulkadir. He forbade us to leave Mogadishu and refused to lend us a car, explaining that every photo Walter might want to take needed a special permit. He complained when Walter played football with my cousins and insisted that I ensure that he behave like a grown-up. I was angry and couldn't understand my uncle's behavior. But finally he allowed us to be driven to Merka, a city just south of Mogadishu, famous for its beaches. Jama, a chauffeur, and a guard went with us; all three carried guns. Nobody told us why those were necessary.

On the first day of the journey, our Land Rover entered a gas station. The chauffeur filled the tank, and Walter pulled out his wallet. The driver then got back into the car and drove off. "Hey!" I called out. "We didn't pay."

"Why should we?" Jama said. "Everything belongs to us anyway."

Walter gave the chauffeur a number of bills and said, *"Stop the car and go back, please."*

"Tell your husband to put the money away," Jama commanded. "He's dishonoring the family."

It didn't take long before we were fighting among ourselves.

Later we reached a plantation. "We'll get you some coconuts," the guard said. So we got out and stretched our legs. A few meters away someone screamed. Suddenly several dozen men, armed with clubs, jumped out of the bush and ran toward us. A hippopotamus was after them! I climbed up on the car's roof. Walter grabbed his camera. Running, he sprinted behind the hippo as the men with clubs cursed and tried to escape it. I almost fell off the roof laughing.

Once the farmers had driven the hippo back to working the irrigation system, they sent a few boys off to climb the palms and bring us coconuts. "Make sure he doesn't pay," hissed Jama. The same thing repeated itself in the hotel, in restaurants, and in the market.

From Merka we drove to Kismayo and reached a border. On one side of the road a number of cars were parked, their interiors being inspected by uniformed men who rummaged through suitcases and bags. Immediately upon recognizing our car, the soldiers opened the gates. "What's going on here?" I asked my brother.

"Let them just try to stop us," Jama answered. "Anyone who tries, I'll shoot."

I was speechless. So was Walter.

Back in Mogadishu, we went out alone and found our way to the market. In the evening we showed Uncle Abdulkadir the masks and animals whittled from driftwood that we were going to take back to Germany as souvenirs. He liked them. "Where did you get them?"

"We bought them from a merchant."

Immediately Uncle Abdulkadir sent his chauffeur to the market. He brought a trembling merchant back with him. My uncle forced the man to return our money, which he did while I protested. My opposition enraged Uncle Abdulkadir: "Your German thinking is absolutely out of place here." Jama scolded me as well.

Were these my relatives? Secretly, Walter and I returned to the market to give the man his money, but—with fear in his eyes—he refused to take it.

One afternoon while I was napping, Walter disappeared, unnoticed by the guard, through the outer door. He meandered along the streets on foot, ended up in a tea house, ordered a mocha, and got to talking with other men. Where was he from? they asked.

"From Germany," was Walter's reply.

"Germany is a good country," the men praised. "Great football players and a strong economy." But what was he doing in Somalia?

"We're visiting my wife's family," Walter answered.

They asked the family's name. Within seconds the entire tea house was empty, except for Walter alone at the table.

Like a puzzle the pieces fell into place. In Munich, I had read in the newspapers that the president's clan robbed, murdered, and stole. The story was about an attempted coup d'état and revolt. I had not believed it. I could not imagine that my relatives would be breaking the law and ruling like tyrants. They were, after all, my family! They were holy to me, and I wasn't going to stand for reporters dragging them in the dirt. As always, when unwilling to accept something, I repressed it. Now I was forced to admit that things were even worse than I could have imagined.

Somalia was a dictatorship.

One day Walter, Khadija, and I drove to the market. The chauffeur maneuvered the car through narrow lanes. Hostile glances followed us. Walter was taunted—as a white man in the company of Somali women, he angered many. At some point the streets narrowed, so we got out and went on by foot. We stopped at a shop selling Somali clothing. Two boys ran after us with insults. Khadija cursed them, and she wasn't understated about it. A man cried, "You whores!" A boy threw a stone. Khadija hit him in the head.

That did it. Chaos followed.

Dozens of men stormed us, exploding from houses and stores,

burying us under an avalanche of insults and curses. Stones flew, more and more stones. We took refuge in a beauty salon. Khadija telephoned for help. Outside a mob raged. We were afraid.

Minutes later the military and police cleared the area. No sooner had the first troops appeared than all vanished into their houses and into corners and lanes clearly used regularly on such occasions.

The committee of elders met. Jama had fallen in love with a divorced, very wealthy woman who, however, belonged to another clan. My brother had to ask the family council for permission to marry, and he would be compelled to accept their judgment. Before the men withdrew for their deliberations, they debated whether or not Walter should be invited to join them. Half wanted him. After all, he was my husband and belonged to the clan. The other half was absolutely opposed: Walter was new and had to prove himself first. Besides, he did not speak Somali.

"We'll get a translator," said one of those in favor.

"Who could that be?" asked the critics.

"Fadumo!"

"A woman in the family council?"

"Impossible!" They all agreed.

Walter, who did not participate, gave his vote to my father, a gesture that angered Uncle Abdulkadir. Negotiations began. Hour after hour passed, while Jama paced back and forth, circling like a nervous tiger. "How can you let others determine your marriage for you?" I asked. "It's your life—your future!"

"Whatever the family decides, I'll have to accept," Jama answered. "I'm not like you."

"What do mean by that?" I asked.

"Well . . ." Jama searched for words. "You've broken the rules. But you're disabled. Everyone's happy that you found a man at all." It was as if he'd hit me in the chest with a club. My husband had never said a word about my stiff, twisted hands and feet, but my own brother considered me an outcast! Something in me suddenly went stone hard.

In the afternoon, Jama was called into the room. Shortly thereafter, he left the house with his head hanging.

Later the family council considered my case. They wanted to organize another wedding, to marry me according to Islamic and Somali tradition. As a woman I was not asked for my opinion, but I spoke anyway. I didn't want it. Walter also explained that he had already married me and didn't have to be married a second time. Enraged, Uncle Abdulkadir turned away. Uncle Omar, his brother, announced that he was going to offer a wedding present anyway: "I'll buy the bride a trunk full of jewels!" He said it just to annoy Uncle Abdulkadir. A few men complained that I didn't deserve wedding presents because, after all, I hadn't brought them all gifts from Germany. My father took the floor and reminded the speaker of the antique Persian pistol Walter had given to the uncle who happened to be complaining the loudest. Uncle Abdulkadir ordered a jeweler to prepare a mountain of gold jewelry for me.

By the end of the fourth week of vacation, I felt exhausted. Walter had been feeling imprisoned. Moreover, he knew he had not been accepted by the men in the family. They had expected him to follow their rules, but he refused to be uncritically deferential toward the elders, to show the respect that especially Uncle Adbulkadir thought was appropriate. I respected my family but shared Walter's attitude.

I was no longer the same young girl who had left Mogadishu. On our trips around the world my husband had often allowed me to look through his camera lens. Thus focused, I had seen a lot of beauty and brilliance, but also unbelievable poverty and misery, usually only a few meters away from the loveliness. Humiliating experiences in Germany had sharpened my sense of injustice. Many discussions with my husband had ripened me into a woman who thought in terms of social good. Perhaps Aunt Madeleine's example—as she invited the poor to eat—had finally taken root in me. Taking out my own trash and washing my own clothes had long been my habit. It was embarrassing, even painful, to recognize how naïve I had been when I had first lived in Mogadishu. Siad Barre was clearly my uncle, an accepted member of the family—and, therefore, one whose politics I could never criticize.

I tried to talk to Jama a few times, but he always avoided serious conversation. I didn't have the courage to address Uncle Abdulkadir, since feelings between us had become tense. My family had power and believed themselves infallible. Every outside attack drove them closer together, hardening them. And it went without saying that little Fadumo from Germany had nothing of value to say.

Sad and worried, I flew back to Munich.

Two folds of skin. In between, smooth flesh. The labia, a little crooked and uneven. A hole.

So that was it.

I had finally wanted to look. I had had absolutely no idea about that part of my body. If I hadn't seen the little girl babies in the family I'd have had no idea of what I used to look like. I examined what the excisor had left over and what Dr. Schmidt succeeded in reconstructing. I tried to imagine the allegedly gigantic, disgusting growths that were supposed to be there. I could not do so. Were a woman's sexual organs really repulsive? Or was that a fiction motivated by fear? I put the mirror down. A stubborn regret took hold of me. They had taken something away from me and I would never experience the feelings of my sexual organs as they would have been.

After the first time Walter and I made love, a wave of relief and pride swept over me. Finally I had become a real woman and wife, had managed to do what was expected of me, and the act had not destroyed me. I had survived! I felt fulfilled. My love for Walter grew, tied up in part with exuberant gratitude. Only much later did I discover desire.

More than anything else, a deep shame barred my way. In the world in which I had grown up, no one talked about intimacy or sex. Even modern, European-influenced people like Aunt Madeleine and

Uncle Abdulkadir merely made allusions. In fact, I was perpetually ashamed of my body for its imperfections, ashamed that I was sleeping with a man. I was even ashamed when I put on a pretty dress. I tried to cover up my malaise by acting silly. I joked around with my husband instead of meeting him as an adult. To discuss sex or take time for foreplay was difficult for me. Years would pass before I truly enjoyed sex. I was grateful to Walter for constantly encouraging me but also for urging me to refuse or signal when I didn't want to have sex, which was terribly hard for me because I didn't want to hurt him. But Walter insisted on my never doing anything unless I wanted to.

I confided my timid discoveries to Dr. Schmidt, whom I asked for guidance and the assurance that I was doing the right thing. I phoned him when I felt depressed or stressed. I felt very close to him, for he had become a substitute father. He heard secrets I would never have shared with my biological father. "Well, how are you getting on?" he'd ask when I came to the office. He wanted to know whether my skin was gaining sensation. He encouraged me. I would grow increasingly sensitive, he promised. He examined me, praising my body: "The tissue has recovered very well." At first I was also ashamed of the praise, but there was no room for such feelings in Dr. Schmidt's office. He allowed me to air all my reservations, no matter how contradictory.

My confidence increased slowly but it increased.

At some point I wanted to know what desire felt like. As I began to explore my body, I found myself not only washing or rubbing ointments on my skin. Rather, my head hardly knew what my hand was doing as I learned how to stimulate myself. Lack of a clitoris made it more difficult but not impossible.

Because it is the seat of desire, the house must be destroyed.

Girls are infibulated so that, once they are women, they may feel no lust. Their sexual desire must be forbidden and so the clitoris must be removed. Thus, circumcision eliminates libido. It is meant to protect female morals. It fences in the drive for sex, making impossible immoral thoughts and actions.

Whatever reasons are deployed—aesthetic (the folds of skin of the labia and clitoris are gigantic and disgusting); hygienic (after infibulation, it's so much easier to wash); medical (stitching precludes noxious excretions)—the goal is clearly the control of a woman's sexuality. Because a woman's sex drive is many times more powerful than a man's, so they say, *gudniin* frees her from its evil power.

Take away the house and you destroy desire.

One year after Walter and I had visited my family, I returned to Somalia alone. Khadija was disappointed, Uncle Abdulkadir insulted. My aunts were worried. "Tell us the truth, child," my great aunt urged. "Did he leave you?"

I had come to make sense of my feelings. Aunt Madeleine's and Uncle Abdulkadir's family had broken up. The villa had been sold. Dissatisfaction was growing throughout the country and I wondered for how long my family could hold on to their power. My sense of home was slipping away.

Shortly after my arrival, I sought out Uncle Abdulkadir for an intimate conversation. Female strangers came and went, but of course Aunt Madeleine was absent. In my eyes, my uncle had betrayed his ex-wife. I knew she blamed him. Vaguely, I also felt responsible for the divorce. But Uncle Abdulkadir avoided me. He was often away traveling. My friendly uncle had become a power-hungry, dissatisfied man. I would have given anything to have him stroke my head as he had when there were no barriers between us. But I was no longer a child. Without uttering a word, each of us chided the other for having changed.

Disappointed that I could not reach Uncle Abdulkadir, I called on Aunt Madeleine, who had her own house and income, although she no longer attended dinners and receptions. I felt sad, knowing she was excluded from certain social circles. To me, Aunt Madeleine was still an impressive woman, and I thought Uncle Abdulkadir had made a big mistake. Still, I had no choice but to return to my uncle's house. Though I loved them both, Uncle

Abdulkadir was my father's brother, and men dominate Somali society. Even small children know they must prefer their male to their female relatives.

I spent long days with my father. Sitting on a bench in the shade, we told each other stories and passed the time. Into the early hours of the morning I gossiped with Khadija, just as we used to do when we were nomad children around the campfire. I visited my brother Ahmed, his wife, and their eleven children. My sisters and brothers questioned me about Germany, for none but Khadija had ever traveled. "Is it true that women in Germany run around naked?" Jama asked.

"I haven't seen any," I answered. "But on the beach and in certain rivers people swim in the nude."

"Really?" Nobody wanted to believe it.

At some point my father called me aside. "Well, my daughter," he said, pulling on his beard while he searched for just the right words. Impatience made my stomach queasy. "You know," my father continued, "children are a gift from Allah." I understood and shook my head. "Is there anything wrong with your husband?"

"Everything's fine, Papa. Walter has to work. That's why I came by myself."

"But you've been married now for quite a long time."

"Pretty soon we'll have children." My father was worried about me. It was impossible to tell him I was using contraceptives.

I spent weeks in the circle of my family. This time I didn't have to translate or negotiate between the warring parties, nor was I made to feel I was neglecting anyone. As I approached the end of my visit, I thought often about inviting Khadija to return with me to Germany. She kept house for Uncle Abdulkadir, managed the servants, cooked, and worried about her brothers, who were glad to accept her care. Khadija sacrificed herself, but no one appreciated her. No one treated her with the respect she deserved. My sister lived like a typical Somali woman. I wanted to end her servitude. I wanted her to learn to read and write, to get an education and develop her abilities. I wanted Khadija to lead a free, independent, and happy life.

My sister only smiled and said, "Our German."

Jama also treated me as a foreigner.

The speech and traditions of my home had not faded for me. In my view I had simply won a few freedoms from another culture.

The day before my departure I visited Uncle Abdulkadir for the last time. I finally asked him about what had been bothering me. "Is it true what the newspapers abroad are printing about Uncle Siad?"

"What are they writing?" Uncle Abdulkadir asked, lighting up the remains of a cigarette stub.

I hesitated. "I don't know if you really want to hear this."

"Out with it." My uncle seemed to be extraordinarily nervous.

"They are writing that Uncle Siad is a dictator who is ruining the country."

"It's all lies! Those reporters for the foreign press are simply jealous."

With that the discussion ended.

We cried for joy when we found out I was pregnant!

It would be a turbulent, demanding pregnancy. Until the end of the fifth month I threw up several times a day and grew even thinner than I already was. At the same time I enjoyed an extraordinary amount of energy. Dr. Schmidt prescribed vitamins and strict bedrest. Like a good girl, I ate fruit, but it was an awful trial for me to lie still on the couch part of the day. Walter had found a larger apartment. We painted the walls and pushed the furniture around. His mother phoned often, asked how I was, and ordered me to take good care of myself. She and I had become more friendly after Walter had threatened to break with her entirely, and now she was clearly ecstatic, waiting for her first grandchild. Nothing was going to stop me now. When a group of right-wingers put up a stand in the pedestrian zone and distributed flyers reading, "Foreigners, get out!" I strode firmly to their booth. A number of men came to my aid. I was lucky—a kick to the stomach could have killed my child. But pregnant women don't always think straight. They think pregnantly, and nothing could have stopped me in those days.

I was a woman, and I was having a baby.

For years I had hated my body, and, as much as I could, ignored it. It had disappointed me and offered nothing but constant pain and problems. It had been skinny and ill, not feminine and pretty. It was never as it should have been. Had I been able to, I would have abandoned that body and slipped into another one. But with my pregnancy my body became the center of my life and the life of my child.

I called Khadija and invited her to visit. "We're sending you a ticket. You'll live with us."

"Oh yes, gladly." Despite the bad connection I heard the happiness in her voice.

"We're going to do the town. Maybe even drive to Berlin."

"Oh yes!"

"Good. I'll call you as soon as we've booked the flight."

"Okay. I'm very happy. Hear from you soon."

Then, for the first time, I awoke in the middle of the night bathed in sweat. I had dreamed that the baby's head had emerged from my body but had gotten stuck halfway. Helpless, I was forced to watch it suffocate. Walter tried to calm me down.

The next night I found myself in the woods, alone in a clearing. Suddenly labor started but the child lay sideways and couldn't come out.

Every night the same kinds of pictures appeared: my womb sewn shut, and the child unable to be born and dying.

Every night brought a chill up my spine and a mad fear.

Then the fantasies started coming by day. Within seconds I was dizzy, trembling, and had to sit down. I saw the excisor's hands and heard the squeaking of the thorns. I smelled the dust and the blood. My memories were sharp and clear. Blue pain seized my legs, pounding them from heels to hips. And suddenly I felt it again, the old separation, the old enmity. My lower body wasn't mine. It had a life of its own and was stronger than I.

Pain moved in as a squatter and stayed. I had only to think of giving birth and my whole body froze. My arms and legs filled with

143

pins and needles, and toward the end even my jaw cramped. I
called Khadija. "Please, come quickly. It could be any day now."
Dr. Schmidt had calculated March 5.

"Ahmed has a cold. I can't leave him alone."

"But Ahmed's wife can take care of him. Besides, it's only a cold!"

"I have to be with him. But I'll come as soon as he's recovered."
I didn't understand my sister. Disappointed, I hung up.

Then March 5 came. And went.

Then March 6—gone.

Then March 7—vanished.

On March 10, a Sunday, I noticed that the skin on my stomach wasn't as taut as usual. Walter called the midwife. She examined
me. "Nothing to worry about," she said. "Your baby is simply taking his time."

Monday morning, my face was gray. Dr. Schmidt sent me to the
hospital. They found an extraordinarily high protein concentration
in my urine as well as alarmingly high blood pressure—two signs of
poisoning in a prolonged pregnancy. The baby's heartbeat was weak.
I was given an infusion of medicine. Two days passed before the doctors ordered a cesarean. "Please, not today," I begged. Walter's father
had died on March 13. I didn't think our child should be born on the
anniversary of his death. The doctors didn't understand.

The anesthesia had not yet begun working when they began
cutting my stomach. It sounded like ripping a heavy cloth. The
pain took my breath away. Then my eyes grew heavy. When I came
to, the nurse put a baby in my arms. "Does it . . ." I asked, still
groggy, "have ten straight fingers?"

When I woke up the second time, baby Philip was gone.

I screamed, cried, and shouted for the nurses—I wanted to see
my child! But Philip had been placed into an intensive care unit in a
children's clinic. The birth had been dramatic. Despite the cesarean
and anesthesia I had pushed with all my force as the anesthesiologist
was putting needles in my thigh. With every push, waves of blood
shot out. I had gone into labor and begun twisting just as the doctors

144

were getting hold of the infant. They finally had to restrain me. I had nearly bled to death. By the time Dr. Schmidt had managed to cut the umbilical cord, Philip's heartbeat had become a mere whisper.

My stomach hurt. I knew the wounds would heal slowly, but truly torturous was having to watch the other mothers with their heavenly smiles holding their newborns and feeding them. Milk streamed from my breasts as I had never imagined. My whole body longed for my son. I agonized over every moment that separated us.

Walter traveled back and forth between the hospitals every day, bringing Polaroids. Daily, he described Philip's tiny advances. The pictures and stories, however, just made me more sad. One day, he said, "Come on. It's noon, and they're all taking a break. I'll drive you over."

We sneaked out of the clinic. Every step was excruciating. I could hardly sit and had to bite my lips when Walter helped me into the car. At every bump I raised my backside to avoid feeling the jolt, but it was impossible to elevate my body without tightening my belly muscles. Everything hurt, and relief came only with the sight of the children's clinic.

I could see Philip through a glass wall.

A nurse held him in her arms and smiled. Rage filled me; I was barely able to contain myself. That was *my* child! That foreign woman had no right to touch him, to cuddle him! Walter escorted me into the room. With shaking legs I bent over my son. Philip looked like an old man, his face wrinkled, his skin thin and transparent as parchment. His eyes looked as though they had already seen a great deal. Tiny and emaciated, he lay in his incubator, needles in his little arms, a tube in his nose. Wires connected him to a screen on which waves rose and fell, only to rise to new heights a second later.

I burst into tears.

When Philip was discharged, he weighed just under six and a half pounds—tiny as a worm. He had a large mouth, perfectly beautiful feet, and the strength of a baby many times his size. He never slept for longer than half an hour. I didn't sleep either. I stopped eating and dropped down to eighty-eight pounds. But day by day my son grew chubbier.

I called Khadija. She cried when I told her she'd become an aunt. "We have a flight reservation for you."

"I'll come as soon as father gets back."

"Why? Where is he?"

"Visiting Uncle Yusuf and his family."

"Is that a good reason not to come?"

"First I have to know that everybody's taken care of here."

"You can call."

"No, I've got to see it with my own eyes. The family needs me."

"I need you, too. You're my sister."

"I'll fly as soon as father gets back." My sister piled up the excuses. I couldn't understand why. I was hurt.

In Somalia, the women in my family would have taken care of me; in Germany, Waris from Augsburg moved in for a week. There really wasn't much I didn't already know about taking care of a baby, but Waris gave me support. Our lives had been turned upside down since the arrival of an infant who seemed never to tire. Still, I missed Khadija and phoned her again, holding the receiver up to the baby's bed where Philip gurgled and cooed. "He's getting more beautiful every day. We named him Philip Jama."

Khadija cried. "You haven't forgotten tradition," she said. Only then did I remember that in my mother's family, every generation named one son Jama. Unconsciously I had continued the legacy.

"You wanted to become an aunt so badly. When are you going to visit your nephew?"

"After the anniversary of mother's death day. Then I'm coming for sure."

But Khadija didn't come. And three weeks after the birth of her grandchild, Walter's mother died.

8

And Somalia burst into war.

TV showed militia—young men with weapons raging through the capital, shooting. We saw refugees, children with faces distorted by fear, and we saw corpses strewn along the roadsides. The news agencies described fighting between guerrillas and the army, massacres and blood baths. Daily, newspapers tallied the wounded and the dead.

Somalia exploded, and all of its hatred and rage poured out over the administration, targeting the entire Marehan clan, my family. A female cousin was caught by marauding rebels, tied to the fenders of two cars, and pulled to pieces. My favorite cousin Saïd and innumerable male family members were killed, the women raped, an aunt stoned. A mine blew up the car carrying my father and other elders of our tribe. All died.

Every time the telephone rang, a part of me died, too.

In the eighties Somali clans had formed their own parties. Somalis in exile had organized political resistance and even within Somalia some dissidence emerged. President Siad Barre ordered federal troops to attack his opponents. Repression led to further assaults. The government began to fight its own people.

Opposition groups constantly splintered, since clans and sub-clans were internally divided. The Somali army dissolved and its soldiers joined tribal militias. In response to a coup d'état, troops loyal to the administration reacted with a massacre. On the basis of clan affiliation alone, people were persecuted and arrested.

Despite different clan membership, more than 100 prominent Somalis joined forces to produce a manifesto calling for a solution to the conflict. The president arrested the manifesto's signatories. During a rally in Mogadishu stadium, Siad Barre was booed. His security forces turned the scene into a bloodbath. Thousands died.

Civil war began.

President Siad Barre fled.

Obsessed, I sought out every newspaper and report, and scrambled to hear any anecdote having to do with my homeland. After Uncle Siad fled, Ali Mahdi Muhammad became the new president, but his party also excluded other clans from the administration. Fighting continued unabated. Conferences and efforts at conciliation failed or talks were canceled. Somalia divided itself into two camps, one led by General Farrah Aidid, a Hawiye, the other by Ali Mahdi Muhammad, also a Hawiye but from a sub-clan. Both were engaged in gunning down my people, the Darod. Everyone fought against everyone else, the government dissolved, and there were bombings, shootings, and killings.

In Somalia, blood feuds reign. Whenever men of one tribe are killed, survivors feel obliged to avenge their deaths by murdering as many members of the offending tribe as possible. Once all the men have been disposed of, it's the women's turn: If pregnant, they risk having their bellies slit to ensure that no child, especially no son, is born. The killing never stops. Only rarely, and for the price of innumerable camels, is a council of elders able to intervene and negotiate an end to bloodshed. Daughters, too, are sold in marriage to the enemy in order to satisfy the demands of a blood feud.

With the last of my energy I took care of our son, building towers out of blocks, singing children's songs, and pushing the baby carriage around the English Garden. As soon as Philip fell asleep, I'd get on the phone. At first I didn't know where to turn. I called Caritas—

a Catholic international humanitarian aid and relief organization—and asked how I could find out who had survived a massacre, who had escaped the mob, and where they had fled. They sent me to the International Red Cross. For hours I filled out search requests, wrote the names of my brothers and sisters on forms, their ages, heights, the burn scar on Khadija's right hand. Nobody knew where Ahmed, Jama, Muhammad, or Khadija had found shelter; no one knew whether they were still alive.

Months passed. I couldn't sleep and stopped eating. Befogged and empty I went about my daily tasks. Guilt weighed me down. Why hadn't I insisted more emphatically that my sister come? She could have been in Germany. Every morning I ran to the mailbox; every afternoon I phoned the refugee commissions. Evenings I sat in front of the TV to watch the marauding soldiers and hired guns turning my country into a pile of rubble.

Then a letter from Khadija arrived.

She was alive! She had fled Mogadishu and made it to Kenya. During the week-long trip she had fallen off a truck and broken fingers and toes. Now she was in a refugee camp. There they had had to amputate her toes. Because of the miserably unhygienic conditions she had also contracted hepatitis. I was relieved, shocked, ecstatic, and desperate.

Later I learned that Jama had survived as well. He had traveled through Kenya to Uganda. Muhammad had fought his way through to Kismayo, a Somali region mainly inhabited by Marehans where he felt relatively safe. Ahmed continued to live with his wife, a Hawiye, in her clan's territory. Her people hid him.

Walter and I sent all the money we had.

In 1992, when ten thousand people had already been killed and thirty thousand had been wounded, a UN delegation met in Mogadishu. But General Aidid refused to negotiate. In New York, the General Assembly passed a resolution appealing to the warlords to end the conflict. An agreement calling for a truce was signed and an embargo launched.

The fighting continued.

Further UN resolutions and an action plan followed. Siad Barre entered the fray once again, sending troops into a city close to Mogadishu, creating another wave of refugees. Ali Mahdi Muhammad called for general mobilization. General Aidid started a counteroffensive. Siad Barre fled to Kenya and then went into exile in Nigeria.

To escape hunger and war, at least five hundred thousand Somalis fled.

At some point my frozen emotions melted. I felt my pain.

I mourned my relations' torturous deaths. I mourned for the women, abducted, raped, and dishonored for life.

And I cried for my father.

The United Nations sent in their Blue Helmets to offer humanitarian aid. Media carried the stories, and other aid organizations discovered the Somali cause. An air bridge was set up to supply the people.

Civil war continued.

Fighting hindered the distribution of food. Pakistani UN soldiers were attacked by Somali warlords. Although the United Nations hired armed locals to protect their convoys, only about a quarter of the intended aid reached its destination.

People were starving.

The United States offered to send twenty-eight thousand soldiers under a UN mandate to Somalia to secure humanitarian aid. For the first time in its history, the United Nations approved a military invasion.

The day UN troops marched in, I was glued to the TV, watching the Blue Helmets on Mogadishu's beach blinded by the flashing lights of the world's press. The men looked as if they couldn't see where they were going.

I hoped they would bring peace.

Uncle Adbulkadir phoned from the Netherlands with news: Idil and Qamaan had traveled from Kenya to the United States;

Saïda was in the United Kingdom, and Ahmed had followed her via a detour through France; and Aunt Madeleine was in Canada.

"I wanted to defend my country," Uncle Abdulkadir said, his voice wavering. "I wanted to fight those primitives." His children had forced him to flee.

Walter and I sent more money. We were now responsible for about fifty relatives who had managed to save themselves but who were destitute and living as refugees. We were reaching our financial and emotional limits.

The telephone never stopped ringing.

My bones ached with rheumatism—my joints swelled again. The tendons gave and the middle knuckles on my fingers slipped. My right hand froze, crooked as a comma, and couldn't be budged. I tried to diaper my kicking Philip using only my left hand. I hung a piece of fabric around my neck, making a sling that allowed me to lift my son out of bed. My neighbors helped me to feed him. The orthopedist suggested an operation, but I refused.

In Somalia, the fighting continued, and my hope for peace vanished. More and more foreign troops marched in, but neither the military nor their governments made any effort to understand the intricate structures and traditions of the country. The soldiers staggered around blindly, caught in a net of feuding clans, of intrigue, enemies, and hatreds, as well as weapons and drugs. Hostilities escalated. Aidid's men killed UN troops, and UN troops took revenge. Washington sent a contingent of four hundred Army Rangers under their own commander to arrest General Aidid. Diplomats and representatives of charitable nongovernmental organizations (NGOs) criticized the UN troops. Eighty American soldiers were injured, eighteen killed. A raging mob pulled their bodies through the dusty streets of Mogadishu. U.S. President Clinton swore revenge.

Some days I would lie down next to my son, press him to me, and take in his sweet baby smell. He gave me the strength to get out of bed.

But the time came when, leaning over Philip's bed, I had a nervous breakdown.

Three years later the Blue Helmets pulled out. Reporters, corre-spondents, photographers, and filmmakers went with them. Mutual massacre by hostile clans continued, but the media aban-doned Somalia.

The world left the country to itself.

I thanked destiny for having spared me firsthand experiences of horror. Yet fear for my relatives never ceased. I tried to repress the terror, but it marched through my mind's back door again and again. I had a family, a supportive husband, and a son. But I lived in a permanent state of anguish. Once again, many months had elapsed since Khadija had written. Was Jama still alive? When I heard about disturbances in Kismayo, I phoned the local UN office. Had the Hawiye found Ahmed in hiding and killed him?

How many deaths would I have to survive?

How many could I withstand?

I sent e-mails to my cousins in the United States and the Unit-ed Kingdom. I called my nieces in Norway. Depressed, they were suffering from the cold, from long days without light. I visited Uncle Abdulkadir, who was edgy and became aggressive when I asked if he really hadn't seen it coming. He spoke constantly about the past. He would talk of nothing else. He reinvented it to suit his fantasies. My uncle had lost everything—family, position, wealth. Rebels now lived in his house in Mogadishu.

He was a broken man.

When Philip was a little older, I agreed to an operation on my right hand. The surgeons put artificial joints in four of my fingers. They were the smallest joints that had ever been implanted. Groups of doctors came to my bedside to examine my x-rays, to make prog-noses, and to pass judgment. Nobody showed any interest in me. Everybody looked at and talked about my hand. I was "the hand" and glad my rear end hadn't needed to be fixed.

Talking to a specialist for internal medicine, I learned that the kind of rheumatism I had was usually provoked by an infection or trauma. Could the trigger have been the festering following infibulation, or even the *gudniin* itself? The doctors couldn't say for sure.

The stitches came out, the wounds healed, and I enjoyed better use of my fingers. But they would remain bent forever. After so many years, I could only be resigned.

In the now-isolated Somalia, feuding clans and their militias drove the country ever closer to disaster. Terror, anarchy, and chaos governed daily life. A whole generation of children grew up in wartime—violence was normality for them. Before they could read or write, they had learned how to handle guns, maraud through the streets, and volunteer as soldiers. They were often paid with drugs. They learned that if you wanted something, you took it. If a boy wanted a man's shirt, he would simply shoot him to get it. Or a man could be shot not for his shirt but for someone's pleasure in killing him. Human life was cheap. Adolescents raped women for fun. Children vanished. Their organs wound up on the international market in exchange for cash.

It was a nightmare.

The world closed its eyes.

I closed mine as well, because it was more than I could bear. Fear gnawed its way into me and stayed. Fear emptied me, gave me headaches, took away my strength. How was I going to explain all of this to my child? For a long time I had hoped to return to Somalia. I wanted my son to meet my family. Philip should see where his mother grew up, should know his other home, should become familiar with his African roots. At some point I had to admit that the road back was blocked. I was a Marehan. They would kill me the moment I set foot on Somali soil.

The country where I was born had disappeared. Somalia had no legitimate government and maintained no political representation in foreign lands. There was no embassy where I could renew my passport. After nineteen years in Germany, I ran the risk of becoming illegal. I decided to apply for German citizenship.

I found the necessary documents and set out to do it. Married for fifteen years and the mother of a child, I could not imagine that the authorities would suspect I was in a marriage of convenience. After I described my problem, the man in immigration and naturalization said, "No problem." I would only need various papers, and my husband would have to trace his German family tree back to 1880. The employee smiled. On his desk stood an African violet.

"I won't be able to show you my parents' birth certificates."

"No?"

"No. Not only do nomads not run to city hall to announce the birth of a child, but in Somalia there is civil war. Official documents no longer exist, since the institutions have been wiped out. Mogadishu is a slaughterhouse."

"That's too bad," the man said, still smiling.

"So what can I do?"

"Nothing," the man said. "Without papers you can't become a German citizen. It's the law."

First I exploded with rage. Then I froze. No documents, no papers—no papers, no existence. A smiling Bavarian administrator had canceled my existence to devote himself, undisturbed, to his African violet.

I managed to collect a police statement of good conduct, all my tax returns, proof of social security payments without any gaps, and all the permits showing that during the past fifteen years I had resided in Germany only. The employee accepted the papers with a smile. A few days later he discovered that, when I had been living with Waris and Detlef in Augsburg, my health insurance had lapsed for six weeks.

"I'm sorry," the employee said.

"What can I do?"

"We'll have to look into the situation. Wait until we get in touch with you."

I waited, called, stopped by, made inquiries. The health insurance documents were scrutinized. The bureaucrat discovered that another, extremely important paper was missing. I brought it over. Suddenly it turned out that one of the certificates had expired. I got a new copy.

"What do I do now?"

"Wait until you hear from us."

"My passport is expiring. In a few weeks I'll be in Germany illegally if my application isn't worked on before then. You've got to help me."

"I'm sorry." The administrator smiled.

Burning with rage I drove home. This particular employee had known me since I had first come to Munich. Yet he still treated me like a criminal. I described the case to one of my husband's colleagues, a lawyer. "It's not at all unusual," he said. "The office is playing for time. They deliberately let documents expire, deadlines pass, and, in the end, years go by before anything is decided." From then on I made sure every document was stamped with the "in" date and insisted that I be given a copy. Still, we remained pressed for time.

Shortly before the deadline I received a letter. The official, using personal discretion granted by his office, had taken it upon himself to reject my application for citizenship. He was not required to give a reason.

The country in which I had lived for so long wanted me out. The ground shifted under my feet. I had no idea what to do. By pure coincidence an editor of the *Süddeutsche Zeitung*, a leading German newspaper, learned about what had happened. The number of cases like mine had been piling up for quite some time. The editor started his research.

Five days later I received another letter.

My citizenship request had been accepted.

For some time I had been working as a volunteer interpreter for refugee organizations. I accompanied Somali refugees to hearings in court and drove to the airport whenever immigration officers detained Somalis without papers. I also went to the airport when people who had been denied asylum were being deported. The work was tiring and often frustrating, but I knew I was doing something worthwhile. It helped me overcome my feelings of impotence. Then I was invited to train as an interpreter in ethnomedicine.

155

Nearly everyone enrolled in the course was female, and nearly all had already worked as translators for years. Many came from Arab countries and Eastern Europe, a few from Africa. A psychiatrist led the group. He explained the concept of ethnomedicine. Even if Germany actively discouraged immigration, practically speaking, increasing numbers of migrants were walking into doctors' offices and hospitals, where they almost always experienced communication problems, not only because of faulty language skills, but also because of different cultural concepts of health, illness, and therapy. For instance, a German doctor had no idea what to think when a patient said, "I have a red pain" or "My body is a desert storm." Or a female patient might not understand why she needed an enema, let alone why it was to be administered by a man. A group of physicians had gotten together to train a circle of interpreters to help bridge such cultural gaps. They recognized that not only money but also lives could be saved when communication between doctor and patient worked well. I felt as though a longstanding tension had been resolved. Soon I was assisting registered physicians who treated Somali patients.

"My body is burning, doctor," a young woman complained. The doctor thought she might be having a stroke and asked her to undress. The woman was shocked.

"My heart is hot," said another. She had gynecological problems, but no Somali woman talks about that part of her body. Instead she might describe heart pain, back pain, abdominal pain.

"There are butterflies in my stomach."

In discussion I found out she had uterine cramps.

I started giving lectures to hospital personnel who often had no idea what ethnomedicine was. I requested that the physicians formulate their questions in ways that would not embarrass their patients. I told them how important it was to recognize that only with time would African women patients develop a sense of trust. I criticized those doctors who forced Somali women, complaining that they had been sullied, to describe in great detail the rapes they had suffered.

The general lack of sensitivity angered me. I told patients

about their right to ask for a female doctor. I fought with the Ministry of Health for recognition of these needs. I insisted that a male interpreter take over when a Somali man had to describe his experiences as the victim of multiple rapes to spare him the humiliation and torment of having to speak of these things in the presence of a female. The Ministry stopped asking for my services. I was ejected from doctors' offices, clinics, and law offices. Still, I refused to shut up. Mine was a deep rage that rushed in torrents. And I was forced to recognize that almost nobody in Germany—with the exception of Dr. Schmidt—knew anything about *gudniin*.

At about this time I read Waris Dirie's *Desert Flower* (1998). Like me, Dirie was born in Somalia and had been infibulated as a child. When her father wanted to force her to marry, she fled to Mogadishu. Later, in London, her beauty was "discovered." After living for a number of years as a successful model in New York, she settled in Vienna, Austria. In an interview with an American journalist, she told her story. For the first time a woman let the whole world know about her circumcision. The report became a cause célèbre: The Western world had had no idea that such a horrific ritual could be so widespread. Following the newspaper report came TV interviews and speeches. Waris Dirie became a special ambassador in the UN campaign against genital mutilation of women and girls.

I swallowed her book whole. It wracked me, made me jubilant, and left me sleepless. When Waris Dirie described her pain, I felt mine all over again. When she screamed, I screamed. I saw myself in her place and lived through situations that were decades behind me. The book moved me as no other ever had.

Suddenly, Germany was talking about FGM. Women friends asked me about my experience, hesitantly at first, then more freely. I talked to acquaintances and neighbors, and got in touch with my friend Waris in Augsburg. It was as if the dam had broken. And yet, it made me angry that the whole world called what happened to me "mutilation." Yes, I was certainly damaged—but "mutilated" referred to casualties of war, someone whose arm or leg had been blown off by a grenade. I was not an invalid. I remained a woman. In a process lasting many years, I had cultivated a friendlier attitude toward my body and had even learned to enjoy sex.

One evening I was flipping through TV programs and heard, suddenly, a child shrieking in Somali: "Mommy! Help me!" I froze. It was as if this cry came from my mouth—as if my own voice were calling. Those had been my exact words. Against my will, my thighs pressed together. The child shrieked and shrieked, and I stared at the screen but saw nothing, my eyes blinded as though someone had just blown smoke in my face. Because my eyes failed to see, my ears heard even more sharply.

At some point pictures on the TV emerged from the fog, showing the operation. I smelled blood, earth. I saw bony fingers, a clearing.

The squeal of a blade through flesh.

Then the camera panned to a group of studio guests discussing female genital mutilation. The moderator invited the audience to participate. A telephone number appeared on screen. As though hypnotized I took in the digits. In my ears the girl's screams continued to sound. One of the studio guests said that genital mutilation is a current practice in many African countries. Every time he pronounced the words "genital mutilation," I jumped. I could have punched him! The first listeners called in. A few were weeping, others angry. A few complained about being faced with such horror as part of their evening's entertainment. I was burning, raging, and dialing the telephone. A voice answered. Words shot out of my mouth; I couldn't think straight. I felt rage and shame and mourning. How could they be so disrespectful? Why show a tortured little girl in the depths of despair if not to appeal to millions of voyeurs? Couldn't they imagine what a child might feel when faced with such an image?

Suddenly realizing how long I had been speaking, I interrupted myself and was about to hang up when the only woman among the studio guests called out, "Wait!" And then she added, "Please leave your telephone number. I'll call you back."

The woman did call back. She introduced herself as Christa

Müller, wife of Oskar Lafontaine and founder of an NGO called the International Action Against Circumcision of Women and Girls—better known as (I)NTACT. We talked for two hours. She said I was courageous, that I shouldn't give up, that I should become more active and fight like Waris Dirie, and, if I needed help, I should phone her.

Euphoric, I began reading books and essays, and searching websites on FGM. I wrote long letters to Christa Müller and received boxes of information in return. But soon I grew impatient with brochures and financial donations. I wanted to become involved in doing something, but did not know how. My euphoria trickled into sand.

Months later I was sitting in front of the TV again. This time the camera followed a woman: Her walk and the way she swung her hands told me she was Somali. Her name was Asili Barre-Dirie. A veterinarian, she was also the vice president of the Foundation for Women's Health Research and Development (FORWARD–Germany), a registered charity that worked to end female genital mutilation. Immediately I knew I wanted to meet her. For days Walter and I tried to locate FORWARD. Finally a telephone number connected me to an answering machine.

Again, I had an empty feeling.

That same evening Tobe Levin, the president of FORWARD–Germany, called. In 1983 a group of African and British women gathered in London and founded FORWARD. The following decade, FORWARD became an international organization. Groups formed in 1990 in California, in 1998 in Germany, and in 1999 in Nigeria. Honorary chair of the German section is a leading feminist author and editor, Alice Schwarzer.

FORWARD campaigns against female genital mutilation. It cooperates with network partners, institutions, and local organizations to inform and care for circumcised women.

One week later, Tobe Levin visited me in Munich. American-born, and bursting with energy, she got straight to the point. "I've brought you a catalog of our traveling exhibition. This winter the pictures are coming to Munich. Could you ask the city's health department to host the exhibition here?"

Finally, there was real work for me to do!

I knocked on doors and explained why an exhibition of paintings against female circumcision was important. I explained how many African women were living in Germany and suffering complications; how education on the issue could protect immigrant children—the ones growing up here. I insisted that government agencies cooperate. It was high time we freed this subject from taboo. I used my contacts in refugee organizations and made my intentions known to everyone on their distribution lists. I phoned Bavarian Television and all the women's magazines, giving the first interviews of my life. I couldn't have been more convinced of the importance of and need for this work. A professional journal asked me to write an article. Amnesty International invited me to give a lecture.

On entering the room, I was shaking. My hands and feet were ice cold. A small redheaded man with freckles greeted me and showed me to my seat. Tables and chairs formed a horseshoe, with the speakers at the head. Relieved to find no podium, I sat behind the sign with my name on it and watched the room fill up. I couldn't utter a word.

The redhead opened the event and presented the speakers. I was sure I was going to throw up. Walter, sitting next to me, held my hand. The audience applauded. The redhead got up. Following his brief introduction, all faces turned to me.

"Hello," I said, clearing my throat. "My name is Fadumo Korn." A man asked me to speak up. I coughed, breathed deeply, and counted to three. "My name is Fadumo Korn," I repeated. "I want to tell you why I am happy to be an African woman. You'll probably wonder about that, since this is a meeting about human rights and genital mutilation, so the fact that I'm happy might come as a surprise." I spoke quickly and without looking up.

"It's true, of course, that I was circumcised. When I was eight, my parents had the excisor come. The woman was old and almost blind, and what happened that morning in the clearing I will never forget. Afterward, when the wound became infected, I developed a high fever and fell into a coma. My family feared I would die. Girls are always dying as a result of circumcision, so it's nothing unusual. People would say, 'Allah has taken the child to himself.'

"Allah let me live. I recovered. But I was never the same again. Formerly a curious, undisciplined, sometimes willful girl, now I withdrew, became silent, and was preoccupied with death. I was infinitely sad and couldn't understand why. My joints swelled, and my fingers and toes became deformed. I was never hungry and grew skinny as a rail. My father brought me to relatives in Mogadishu. Years went by before I was diagnosed with rheumatism. Then my family sent me to Germany for therapy.

"Here I was fortunate to find a country with good doctors and clinics. I was treated and operated on. My pain was eased although I can't be cured. I'll have rheumatism for the rest of my days, but I've accepted it because, despite my handicap, I can live a happy life. I got to know my husband. I met a sensitive physician who opened me up. Both supported me in becoming a woman who likes her body and is able to enjoy sex. I'm eternally grateful for that and want to share my happiness. For women who went through a similar trauma, I want to be an example and source of support. And I want to prevent what is happening daily: little girls being subjected to this horrible custom. If I can save even one little girl, the effort will have been worthwhile. So you can see . . ." For the first time I became conscious of myself in the room and took in the listening faces. "You can see, that's what I meant by the happiness of an African woman. Thank you."

For a moment, there was perfect silence. Then a few people began to applaud. Others joined them. The applause grew louder and became an avalanche. The redheaded man got up; came over to me, and held out his hand. "Congratulations." Exhausted and happy, I thanked him.

The exhibition opened at the beginning of January in the Ministry of Health. Four hundred people appeared. Representatives of another association, also opposed to female circumcision, had hung posters in the lobby. A few of their members asked for contributions. Reporters interviewed them. It looked as though they were the organizers of the event. Asili Barre-Dirie and I were practically overlooked.

A representative of the municipal Minister of Health gave the opening speech, which flowed into a discussion with various experts. A few women activists took the floor. They attacked female genital mutilation, wallowed in bloody details, preached about underdeveloped cultures, brutal customs, and lack of education. At first I found it embarrassing. These women were talking about me, and what they were saying made me ashamed. But then I got angry and took the floor myself.

"You are absolutely right, honored colleagues. Circumcision of girls is cruel, and it should be opposed. But you are being cruel as well when you, as Europeans, place yourselves above Africans and present them as stupid puppets of an archaic culture. You don't know the real meaning of circumcision, and, of course, you're fortunate not to. But you also don't realize what it feels like when a group of well-meaning folks comes along and talks about you as though you were an object that needed care. Please don't speak for people about whom you really know nothing. It would be better—I'll say it directly—if you shut up."

I made friends and enemies that evening. I learned that you've got to beat your drum loudly if you want to be heard. And I knew that I'd found a home with FORWARD.

To further intercultural understanding and ensure sensitivity, the constitution of FORWARD-Germany mandates that two thirds of its board members be of African origin. Members must also support FORWARD's explicit opposition to racism.

To talk about customs deeply rooted in tradition and culture requires trust. Asili Barre-Dirie flies regularly to Somalia. The women she sees there know and respect her, since she is an accomplished woman. And she shows respect for them too. For that reason, they listen to her and are willing to accept challenges to the fundamental ideas organizing their lives.

FORWARD helps in practical ways. In Shilabo (Ogaden, Ethiopia), the association contributes to running a poultry farm. Village women receive hens whose eggs support the family. True, the men are only too willing to lean back, relinquish responsibility, and let the women do the work. But the women profit. They barter among themselves and improve their negotiation skills, thereby increasing their independence.

FORWARD contributes to girls' education by paying for textbooks, uniforms, and regular health examinations. The association supports families, enabling them to send their daughters to school rather than to herd goats. The mothers, above all, are proud of their school-going girls even though they have not been cut. Funding is offered in exchange for parental promises not to infibulate.

Only a small number of families, however, have taken this difficult vow. Most parents do not see progress in leaving their daughters uncut, although they agree that education is progressive, the path toward a better future.

It wasn't my aim to shock or condemn. Rather, I wanted to win allies who support our common goal. Yet I often slipped into situations that provoked an emotional response.

One Monday morning at eight o'clock I faced the assembled staff of a Munich gynecology unit. I had often been told, I said, that infibulated women were sewn shut again after giving birth. Then I described in gruesome detail how, for half of each month, I used to double over with cramps; how during every menstrual period, I would spend at least three days throwing up; how the blood barely escaped, drop by drop, through a tiny opening; and how it would often close, thus damming the flow of menses so that my stomach ballooned. "Can't you see that it's liberating for a woman to come to Germany and find a doctor to open her up?" I looked into a sea of closed faces.

"Can you imagine how relieved these women feel?"

Nobody said a word.

"But sometimes," I carried on, "after a woman bears a child, the physician stitches her shut."

Silence.

"Doctors violate the interests of a patient simply because a husband waiting in the hallway says, 'Please close her up again.'"

Silence. Some in the audience were looking out of the window.

"We know of such cases here in Munich. Therefore, I'm calling on you, in case you're asked to restitch, to refuse. Do it in the woman's best interest. She's already suffered enough. Explain to the man that, in Germany, it's forbidden."

"I'm not going to stick my nose in somebody else's affairs," one physician offered. He wore a determined expression.

"I'm not going to destroy a family," chimed in another.

"Can't you simply stitch what's medically necessary," I asked, "and spare the woman additional agony?"

"If I don't do it, somebody else will," he answered.

I gulped.

"What do you suggest?" a very young doctor asked. "After all, it's tradition. You can't simply say 'no.'"

"There are associations that oppose female circumcision and offer seminars for medical personnel. I'd be happy to help you organize such a training session for your colleagues."

A woman doctor rose to leave. "During a birth I have to make quick decisions," she said, buttoning her white coat. "I don't have time for deep reflection."

"But . . ." I began, trying hard to keep my voice calm and friendly. "You have taken an oath that obligates you to consider the patient's best interest. You don't have to act on a third party's wishes." The woman doctor left the room, and a couple of her colleagues followed.

Again and again I would hear about African families flying their daughters to Egypt or Kenya during summer vacations. There, on holiday, the girls were cut. I spoke in schools and asked teachers to observe their pupils. I tried to sensitize pediatricians, asking them, should suspicion arise, to contact FORWARD, (I)NTACT, or Terre des Femmes—all nonprofit organizations that fight for women's human rights. I told them that we could succeed in convincing parents not to infibulate their daughters.

In the meantime, I had heard that such operations were also taking place in Germany. I didn't have any proof. But I knew that many Africans immigrants were prevented from leaving the country by their conditional residence status. So the rumors were not hard to believe, even if it was difficult, if not impossible, to go behind the scenes. Had I confronted parents directly, they would have closed the door in my face, and I would never have seen their daughters again. Such situations made me furious. I felt tempted to threaten the parents. I wanted them to know that I knew what they were planning and that I could go to the police and bring them to trial.

But then the child might be taken away from her family.

Would that have been better?

I became known. Sometimes Somalis landed at Munich airport and asked for me by name. This surprised but also helped me.

African refugees whom I assisted in Germany had a number of problems, the aftermath of circumcision only one among them. I took the time to know my clients, brought gifts when I came to see them—clothing, CDs, a radio—as you do in Africa. I cultivated trust. That I spoke Somali and looked Somali was of immense importance. Among crowds of strangers, I was one of them, a sister.

As time passed, our talk could move to intimate topics. Women told me about their wedding nights and about giving birth. With surprising good humor, we spoke for hours about *gud-niin* without ever uttering the word at all. They asked me for help when they were in pain. I accompanied them on visits to female gynecologists who had volunteered to work with FORWARD. For fifteen euros—or about nineteen dollars—a woman could have an operation to be opened. Others had to be treated because they had tried to open themselves.

Often I had to assure frightened women that a medical examination wasn't shameful. I informed them about German law that protected them and their children. Although I framed circumcision as a custom we must abandon, I tried not to stand above them, separate from their suffering and their daughters'. Yes, while the tradition deserved to be opposed, people who had obeyed tradition should feel my respect. I wanted to give women and men the opportunity to understand that they were damaging their daughters when they had them cut and sewn. After all, it had taken me quite awhile, despite my suffering, before I began to see myself as someone other than a child chosen by God for purification, living in a country of the impure and unclean.

My mother had caused me pain. But she had no choice. I have never reproached her. It has never influenced my love for her. I had focused all my rage, despair, shame, vulnerability and hate on the excisor. It was important to me that my mother be absolved of blame. To have thought otherwise would have been a deadly sin.

The sharpest critiques of my work came from men. After word got around that I acted as a translator for refugees, increasing numbers of Somali men came to my speeches. On arrival, they knew only my name. As soon as they heard that I was going to talk about *gudniin*, they left the room, accusing me of heresy and betrayal.

"Nowhere in the Qur'an is it written that children should be circumcised," I told them. "Isn't it heresy when I cut part of Allah's work? Doesn't that mean I'm unhappy with what he's made—that I place myself above creation?" The men remained silent, and some appeared ashamed.

But they also stopped inviting me to Somali community celebrations. Some men insulted me on the phone and tried to intimidate me. Then I found two and then three influential Somali men who did support me, once they understood how much suffering the custom caused. One day I asked them to call a meeting of Somali men resident in Munich. As I entered, the room broke out in whispers. At least sixty had come. As the only woman, I stood facing them. I told them there was nothing I wanted from them but that perhaps I had something to offer. If they agreed, I would help them in any way I could. After all, I knew my way around and had useful contacts. "Whoever wants my help has simply to ask. I'm at your service." They all listened silently. "And please," I continued, "stop talking about me behind my back. I know that in your eyes I'm working against tradition. But you must realize that I am now a German woman, and the laws of this land protect me and my work."

I thanked them for coming and left.

Later my supporters reported the discussion that followed:

"She's not a bad woman," several noted.

"She's a Darod," others replied.

"And what's even worse," still others called out, "she's a Marehan, a member of the old regime."

"She was sixteen when she left Somalia," my supporters interjected.

"So what," those opposing me responded. "She's a spy, collaborating with the German government. She's a traitor to our people!"

My supporters negotiated, conciliated, spoke well of me. I refused to be cowed. I went on with my work.

Infibulation is traumatic and can bring lifelong pain.

But you can learn to live with it.

That's a point I constantly stressed in my speeches.

Even after *gudniin*, a woman can lead a fulfilling life. In some respects, it's hard to do, of course, and it's a pity to struggle to achieve what we should enjoy naturally and easily—love for our bodies and sexual pleasure.

But African women are strong.

Epilogue

He was a pilot flying the next day to Nairobi. We met at one of my lectures near Stuttgart. I asked him if he would take a package to Khadija. He said, "Of course."

Quickly I sped back to Munich, looked for a couple of photos, recorded a cassette, and put cash into an envelope. We had been forced to cut back on our spending, and for a while I had sent Khadija only irregular sums of money and medicine.

The next day I gave my package to the pilot. He flew that afternoon. Two days later, on June 7, 2001, he gave my gift to my sister in Kenya.

The evening of the same day friends visited Walter and me in Munich. We cooked and, because it was very warm, ate out on the balcony. In the middle of the night, I suddenly awoke. I woke up my friend as well. Although it was 1 a.m., I asked her to walk out with me.

We strolled down the street and turned onto a path that led to the Isar River. Everything was quiet except for the gurgling water. Stars blinked, and the water shone black. We skirted the shore heading toward the waterfall. I felt nervous and walked as though driven by some indescribable force. My friend followed me, silent. I said little as well. I simply wanted to go on and on, never to stop, as though I would collapse if I paused, as if the restlessness could destroy me.

We reached the waterfall and stood silently watching it crash. It rumbled in my ears. And suddenly I felt relieved and free.

"Let's go back," I said. My friend turned. I put my arm through hers and tried to talk against the silence, but we were both too tired. As we climbed back up to the street, it occurred to us that we hadn't carried any money or a cell phone. "Just think, if anything had happened to us—" I said. We walked faster and were soon home. I crawled back into bed and slept like a happy child until morning.

As we were eating breakfast, the telephone rang.

Khadija was dead.

My sister passed away on the very day the pilot had given her my package. Without anything to kill the pain, she had suffered and died from cirrhosis of the liver following a hepatitis infection.

I put down the phone and went numb.

At night I paced through the apartment, haunted.

When the pilot returned, he gave me a letter and two bracelets from Khadija. In my hands, they were aflame. They branded themselves into my flesh.

I had been too late.

Afterword
FGM: A Note on Advocacy and Women's Human Rights

Wearing the traditional dress of their native countries, a group of African women in London holds signs that read "We Condemn FGM!" They have gathered in 1992 in front of city hall in the borough of Brent to protest the motion by an African woman counselor to legalize female circumcision. "Female circumcision is child abuse," one demonstrator says. "It degrades women and we *vehemently* oppose it." "That's right," Comfort Ottah, a midwife and activist for FORWARD, shouts over other voices. Having encountered "a child who was mutilated," she explains, "the girl wasn't strong enough to go against her parents but the government could have protected her. . . . It hurts my heart very badly, for this isn't cultural, it's torture, and these children suffer for life" (Walker and Parmar 1993a). In *Born in the Big Rains*, Fadumo Korn also calls what was done to her "torture." But like many anthropologists, she views the term "mutilation" with distrust. Why? Between cultural relativists, leery of judgmental terms and advocates of women's human rights, what are the lines of debate?

Many well-intentioned Westerners, aware of colonialist abuses, feel unable to "take sides," because to do so would be dictating what insiders must manage for themselves. I'm convinced, however, that silence is collusion, and that it becomes less difficult to know whose side you are on once you are reminded of exactly what Somali and other African girls are forced to endure. In charting the course of her emerging activism, Fadumo's memoir may help readers to support the abolition of female circumcision. Korn's childhood experience makes the suffering palpable.[1]

While terror pervades Korn's key experience, her words are those of the small child trying to please her mother and the tradition she feels part of. Although the sun has not yet risen, the seven-year-old begins "to sweat" even before an "ancient" woman in a "torn" and "dirty" garment advances into the clearing. The excisor, whom the mother welcomes with "respect," fails to greet the initiate or acknowledge her with so much as a glance later on—another observation Korn remembers. The child both resents being ignored and senses something unpleasant about to happen, so she thinks of her soon-to-be tormenter as "a witch . . . most certainly a witch" (37).[2]

Fadumo Korn's childhood memory also retains a vivid image of the instruments placed before her: "a little sack of ash, a rod, a small metal container with herbal paste, thorns from a bush . . . elephant hair [and] a razor blade [broken] into two halves" (37–8). Furthermore, like many who have undergone this procedure,[3] Korn remembers the cutter's eyes, "heavy-lidded," possibly suggesting impaired vision. She also describes her fingers' agility in wrapping "sisal cord around the [razor half inserted into a slit in the rod so that] it look[s] like a little ax" (38).

Not surprisingly, the child "want[s] . . . to run away" (57). But she also wishes to avoid "sham[ing]" her clan. She has no choice but to submit to this procedure—without any kind of anesthesia, of course—whose aftermath would, in Fadumo's words, determine everything else in her life (quoted in Schuhler 2005).

A voice said: "Hold her tight!" A hand gagged my mouth.
The first cut was ice cold.
. . . deep blue . . .
A lightning bolt to the head. (38)

Fadumo faints from the "all consuming, devouring pain"—and has a typical near-death experience, "floating and looking on from overhead, seeing [herself] on the ground, on the upside-down tub, stiff as a board, [her] mother and Aunt Asha holding [her] tight, putting a block of wood in [her] mouth, and an old woman squatting between [her] legs, carrying out her barbaric craft" (39). The block of wood is often used, even in "milder" cases of clitoridectomy, to prevent the girl from biting off her tongue.

Are tongues, at least figuratively, also amputated? The loss of language appears to be an intended consequence of genital cutting. Fadumo writes: "A shriek to the ends of the world wanted to escape but stuck in my throat" (38). While Fadumo's narrative is born of blue-black pain, a change in her personality follows, the experience effectively silencing her. Not unlike victims of trauma, a muted, timid, introspective person replaces the earlier vivacious spirit.[4]

Fortunately, as this volume makes explicit, Fadumo has emerged from muteness into speech. As vice-president of FORWARD–Germany, she raises funds to support educational, income-generating, and consciousness-raising projects being run in Germany and Africa. Yet, despite her own charismatic public presence, her concern for how to discuss FGM remains acute.

Therefore, "what do you call it?"—FGM, cutting, circumcision?—remains an important question. "Hardliners"—who use "female genital mutilation"—have received welcome support from Senegalese Ousmane Sembene's stunning film *Moolaadé* (2004), awarded first prize at Cannes in the category "Un certain regard" and called "a manifesto against genital mutilation" (Annas and Busch 2005). Sembene, unequivocal in his opposition, follows the NGO community, committed to the term FGM as codified in international conventions crafted by African women and men. And Fadumo agrees with him: "Mutilation" is an accurate description of what was done to her, but she rejects being referred to as a mutilated personality.

Still, in a sense, the dilemma itself is misleading and depends to a great extent on audience. Not "what do you say?" but "to whom?" and "in what language?" are the real issues. At one of its first meetings in 1998, the European Network for the Prevention and Eradication of Female Genital Mutilation (EuroNet FGM) spent an entire day on this subject. Zahra, a Somali in the Netherlands, said: "When I'm speaking to the immigrant community, I use *gudniin* [translated as "female circumcision"]. It's not a problem." Others agreed: Individuals use any number of customary, if figurative and euphemistic designations in their own languages. For example, Ibo novelist Flora Nwapa uses a euphemism, "the bath" (Erben 2000). In Sembene's film, shot in Burkina Faso, we hear *bolokoli*. In Mali, the common phrase is *femmes assises sous le couteau*, or "women sitting under the knife" (Gillette and Franjou 1995; Erben 2000). *Takhoundi* is the word in Sarakolé, *tukore* in Senoufo, both spoken in Mali (Sahel Initiative 2000). Different languages prefer different descriptors. But when individuals address Westerners?

It is certainly true that journalists and others often sensationalize genital cutting. Outrage, if not racism, replaces reason, and a sadistic titillation may also be at work. Certain approaches to the subject can indeed be painful, embarrassing, or humiliating for women who have suffered the procedure. Yet silence is not the alternative. Nor is hiding behind misleading or ineffective language. "Circumcision," for instance, draws a false analogy to male circumcision and diminishes the harm done to women. FGM is not equivalent to the removal of a foreskin (although that too is now opposed by a growing movement[5]). Women's "circumcision," moreover, causes perilous short- and long-term health risks in which scar tissue compromises a fulfilling sex life and threatens the well-being of babies ("Female Genital Mutilation and Obstetric Outcome" 2006, 1853–41). Ultimately and significantly, moreover, the lesson is subordination.

Given growing awareness of the procedure's medical damage, one must conclude that behind the debate about terminology lurks women's subordination. Despite some success,[6] FGM stubbornly persists. In my view, the diaspora itself contributes to the practice's longevity outside of Africa. Genital mutilation is closely associated with ethnicity, challenged by the Western nations' contemporary liberal stance as well as earlier efforts by colonial powers to suppress the practice. Because women are less powerful than men, they can be viewed as "scapegoats of culture and cult" (Levin 1986). In her interviews with Somali immigrants in Switzerland, Charlotte Beck-Karrer found grounds to fear that "*gudniin* is becoming a means of maintaining ethnic and cultural identity [abroad]" (1996, 120). A scene in Fadumo's memoir suggests how deeply young girls connect their sexual bodies and their cultural identities.

While diplomatic parents sip cocktails on a Mogadishu terrace, Somali girls confront their European classmates, taunting them for being wet, smelly, or worse. Although the Spanish youngsters insist, ironically, "We're circumcised like you!" Fadumo declares, "I don't believe it" and escalates doubt into assault. When the Spanish sisters refuse to "prove it," the Somalis unzip and exhibit the bridge between their thighs.[7] When the Spaniards don't do likewise, they are thrown onto the bed and their panties removed.

"Look at them!!" Fadumo cries. "How wrinkled they are, how shriveled, how ugly. Yuck!"

When analyzing this scene, one remembers that Fadumo—now leading the aggressors—was once seized and constrained by women. Fadumo's violent behavior may be understood as validating the admittedly excruciating rite she has endured. FGM's power, I believe, derives from its status as inheritance, a transformative act passed on through the generations. As former chief advisor to WHO's programs against FGM, Efua Dorkenoo attests, "It's not just the cutting of a woman's genitals; it's also the symbolic power of it [with] implications for . . . psychology and character development. Therefore male-dominated society sees any attempt to change it as a threat" (qtd. in Walker and Parmar 1993b, 249). Fadumo's narrative conveys this deep emotional investment in genital erasure. For even if vaginal torture originates in the (imagined) aesthetic preferences of men, women who prefer infibulation self-police the practice to ensure its continuity. "I will certainly circumcise my daughter," a patient tells gynecologist Nawal

Nour in Boston who, like Fadumo, hopes to talk her out of it (Nour 2006). Persuasion has proved difficult, however, for the behavior of those in diaspora remains in thrall to pre-immigration experiences rooted in village or nomadic life and the acceptance by daughters of their mothers' example. In addition, FGM makes manifest an ideal of cultural beauty for parents who want to ensure the perception of their daughters as desirable marriage partners.

To become a "positive deviant" then—that is, to become an activist—means moving from pride to shame to an emotionally neutral knowledge from which opposition may follow. But this difficult psychological maneuver takes enormous courage. At risk are a person's reputation in a community and her self-esteem. In diaspora, activists like Fadumo skirmish on two fronts, with their own people and with their host society. Hence, Fadumo reacts with hostility to the man on the talk show when he mentions "mutilation." Like many victims of FGM addressing the "West," Fadumo refuses to be seen as a "mutilated" cripple, which is what she senses in the talk show participant's stance. She also rejects being spoken for.[8] At Fadumo's first public appearance for FORWARD, opening an exhibition of Nigerian paintings against FGM in Munich's municipal Ministry of Health, the critical tone of Western speakers from another NGO, seemingly without noting the pressures on women to accept genital surgery, makes Fadumo lose patience and tell the allies to hold their tongues. Thus the task of fighting FGM challenges activists to convince policy-makers and foundations that an alarming public health menace deserves to be met with impressive sums for research, prevention, and health care facilities. At the same time these activists must never violate the dignity of victims.

Fortunately, international instruments bearing the impeccable stamp of African authorship codify and thereby propagate an understanding of "female circumcision" as mutilation and, therefore, as a practice that should be addressed with urgency and funds. These include the Maputo Protocol on the Rights of Women in Africa. Adopted by the African Union in 2003, Article 5, paragraph B calls for "prohibition, through legislative measures backed by sanctions, of all forms of female genital mutilation."⁹ Similarly, the UN Declaration on the Elimination of Violence against Women acknowledges the need to eliminate FGM. Article 2 states: "Violence against women shall be understood to encompass, but not be limited to (a) . . . female genital mutilation and other traditional practices harmful to women" (Sen, et. al. 1993). In 1996, the U.S. Congress also passed a law against FGM, as have the majority of African and Western nations with relevant immigrant populations (Rahman and Toubia 2000).

If, then, significant constituencies support abolition, why then the need to discuss terminology? Is it not a distraction from central concerns? Controversy about "what to call it" derives in part from an accidental circumstance, the brusque tone and male-bashing behind early abolition efforts of the late Fran Hosken (1920–2006), who coined the term "FGM." Hosken was the first vocal Western feminist to speak, write, and act tirelessly against the practice. She made the struggle to end excision her life's work. *WIN News*, a quarterly Hosken edited, carried reports on FGM in every issue from 1975 to 2003. Hosken also produced and distributed a teaching tool, the *Childbirth Picture Book* (2000), and in 1979 was keynote speaker at the first international conference on FGM held in Khartoum, Sudan with mainly African participation. Her encyclopedic work, *The Hosken Report* (1993), continues to be cited frequently.

The problems with Hosken's initiative, however, surfaced in an explosive way at the 1980 UN Mid-Decade for Women Conference in Copenhagen. As the *Boston Globe* phrased it, "sharp-tongued and headstrong," Hosken was "accused by anthropologists of committing cultural genocide by criticizing Africans for countenancing female circumcision. She was undeterred by such criticism, [however], having visited hospitals where the practice was not only routine, but subsidized by U.S. aid" (Kahn 2006). Hosken protested this link between U.S. taxpayers and the violation of women's and girls' human rights. In the late seventies, she also wrote to the United Nations Children's Fund (UNICEF), the United Nation's Educational, Scientific, and Cultural Organization (UNESCO), and the World Health Organization (WHO), asking these influential institutions what they were doing to stop the practice. Her actions had a significant impact on organizing work in Germany.

As Germany's leading activist today, Fadumo cooperates with UNICEF, WHO, the *Gesellschaft für Technische Zusammenarbeit* (Society for Technical Cooperation), a technical arm of the German Development Agency that provides international aid, and other governmental agencies. Unlike the deaf ear these institutions turned to Hosken's pleas in the 1970s, all have become involved in eradication efforts and often invite Fadumo to speak. For instance, to celebrate March 8, International Women's Day, UNICEF requested that Fadumo come to Zürich for a week's campaigning, including Swiss television appearances, and then attend a major conference in Berlin's Friedrichpalast opened by Chancellor Angela Merkel on May 15, 2006. Participants included Eva Luise Köhler, wife of German President Horst Köhler, who is patron of the umbrella organization INTEGRA that unites twenty German anti-FGM nongovernmental organizations, and UNICEF international ambassador Vanessa Redgrave. Fadumo is also in touch with Austria's Minister for Health and Women, Maria Rauch-Kallat, presently chairing the European Union Council. The two are prepared to reintroduce the issue in Brussels.

To address the next generation of immigrants and their European peers, the European Union has already allocated funding for several projects managed by EuroNet for girls or young people of both sexes under the DAPHNE program's IDIL[10]—an acronym for "Instruments to Develop the Integrity of Lasses." Fortuitously, the word "idil" means "intact" in Somali. From 2001–2003 IDIL (www.eu-idil.org), in six European countries, attempted to stop FGM in immigrant communities by targeting youth.[11]

In Denmark, for example, Ambara Hashi Nur of the Somali Women's Association (SWOD) in partnership with the Federation of Somali Associations (FSAN, the Netherlands) and the Islington Training Network (ITN, UK), ran "IFT I IN"—Somali for "enlight-

178

enment." African girls, recruited in schools or located through the recommendations of parents, counselors, or religious leaders, met on Fridays to cook, try on make-up, listen to music. But counselors also raised issues of health and beauty that led to debates on FGM. Original to SWOD is the use of empowerment tools such as forum-theater as well as "appreciative inquiry," which means participants interview each other to elicit stories of success. The theory proposes that positive experiences will build the confidence of girls and thus enable them to oppose parents and community: that is, to stop infibulation. Theater professionals polished the girls' stories into stage plays in which participants acted before community audiences. Both a DVD and a comic book have been produced (*Dariatou*, n.d.).

FORWARD–Germany's girls' project, awarded the Gräfin zu Solms Human Rights prize in 2002, has similar confidence-building aims. As managing director, Dr. Asili Barre-Dirie explains: "Unlike their mothers who grew up before exile in a proud culture that taught them self-esteem [based on their ethnicity], expatriate girls, lacking cultural confidence, often react with ambivalence to media distortions" of FGM. Asili's "contemporaries' pride in themselves and their background," she avers, "enables them to single out isolated aspects of tradition, to criticize and improve it" (Levin 2005, 290).

With the aim of ameliorating harmful customs, as well as softening the pain occasioned when German schoolmates criticize African culture, FORWARD–Germany invites girls of Somali origin, ages 14 to 22, to spend several weekends together. With Somali and German counselors, the teens cook, hike, dance, perform, and watch videos on FGM. They also talk about "what it's like to be a black girl in a white world, criticize male family members, demand more personal freedom, ask for sex education, and wish for improved relations with older women in the family" (Levin 2005, 290–291). Fadumo's figurative offspring, these immigrant daughters are becoming the avant-garde of change.

Tobe Levin

June 2006

Waltham, Massachusetts and Frankfurt, Germany

NOTES

1. At a book signing in Munich and again in performance with Alice Schwarzer on February 11, 2005, at FORWARD's "International Zero Tolerance to FGM Day" in Frankfurt, Fadumo retold her infibulation story by reading aloud from her memoir. In fact, the story is performed at every reading (see Schuhler 2005).

2. This detail is not innocent: Alice Walker, an "outsider," was criticized above all else for her "demonization" of the cutter, but often, the victims themselves apply the metaphor. In *L'excisée* by Evelyne Accad (1982), *Mutilée* by Khady (2005) and many other fictional works on FGM, as well as innumerable factual accounts, the excisor appears as a sorceress. See my analysis of Accad in *Comparative American Studies* (2003) and of Walker in Germany in *Black Imagination* (1999b).

3. Dr. Muthoni Mathai, FORWARD activist, working as a psychiatric social worker in Kenya, describes a case in which the excisor was almost blind (Levin 2003, 289). The practitioner's eyesight is frequently in doubt.

4. Not only the larynx but also the ears are assaulted by these operations. Just as Fadumo writes about scraping and scratching, Edna Adan Ismail told me that sixty years later, she can still hear the knife's tearing of her flesh. And another testimony is Nura Abdi's:

When my turn came, I burst into tears [and] screamed, "I don't want to!" [but] that didn't help at all. They grabbed me, dragged me to the empty orange crate and sat me down on it. I screamed, kicked, and was held down on all sides. . . . [When] the *halaleiso* . . . started to cut, there was a sound like sharp scratching or ripping, like knifing a burlap sack or heavy-meshed towel. . . . I was in such shock that no scream came out. No matter what they cut, every time that horrendous scratching jack-hammered in my ear, louder than all the [attending women's] screams.

But the worst was yet to come . . . when they sew you up.

. . . It was as if with all my senses, wholly conscious, I was being slaughtered. I tried to defend myself, but what can a four year old do against six grown-up women? Maybe I moaned, maybe I gasped for breath. But I didn't scream, for I was spared the gag. And then I fainted.

Before they began to bind me up, I came to. It was a new pain this time, the *halaleiso* rubbing herbs on the fresh wound. These herbs are supposed to speed up healing. It felt like I was being held over an open fire.

Again I fainted. (See my translation Abdi and Linder 2003)

5. For further details on the movement against male circumcision see NOCIRC (http://www.nocirc.org/).

6. In response to this sort of social pressure, Gerry Mackie offers a theory of "critical mass": convince a large enough percentage in the same marriage pool to change its preferences simultaneously and one important argument—that to get a husband, a woman must be cut—becomes invalid. Mackie draws a convincing

parallel between conditions permitting the sudden end to foot-binding—after 1,000 years, changed in a single generation—to lessons drawn from TOSTAN's successful campaigns. These include societies, public renunciation, and a critical mass within the marriage pool.

7. Anthropologists' accounts confirm that it is not unusual for Somali girls to settle disputes by comparing their genital scars. For instance, "several times a week you can see girls in a crowd, checking each other's circumcisions. . . . When a girl your age or older calls you sharmuuto, you compete right there, no matter where you are, by taking off your underpants and spreading your legs and letting everyone see if you are a virgin or not" (Barnes and Boddy 2004, 76).

8. After running continuously from February 2000 through February 2006 in Germany and elsewhere in Europe, the exhibition opened in the USA at Brandeis University on 6 April 2006. Catalogues are available from Tobe Levin, levin@em.uni-frankfurt.de.

9. Protocol to the African Charter on Human and Peoples' Rights on the Rights of Women in Africa, adopted by the 2nd Ordinary Session of the Assembly of the Union, Maputo, CAB/LEG/66.6 [Sept. 13, 2000]; entered into force Nov. 25, 2005. See the *African Human Rights Law Journal* 2001.

10. Administered by the Centro Piemontese di Studi Africani in Torino, IDIL covered projects in Italy, Spain, Denmark, Belgium, the Netherlands, and Germany. DAPHNE is a European Community program based on a decision of the European Parliament to prevent and fight violence against women and children and to protect the victims in risk groups.

11. In its *Final Report on Female Genital Mutilation* (2001), the European Parliament Committee on Women's Rights and Equal Opportunities estimates about 270,000 women sufferers or girls "at risk" in Europe. Of these, the UK is home to 30,000, Italy to 28,000, and Germany to 20,000 (Africa Women's Organization, 4). Sweden, Denmark, Spain and, of course, France also host considerable affected populations.

WORKS CITED

Abdi, Nura and Leo Linder. 2003. *Tränen im Sand*. Bergisch-Gladback: Verlagsgruppe Lubbe. Excerpted as "Watering the Dunes with Tears." Trans. Tobe Levin. In *Feminist Europa. Review of Books*. http://www.ddv-verlag.de/issn_1570_0038_jahr2003.4_vol01_nr01.pdf. 28–33. Accessed 31 July 2006.

Accad, Evelyne. 1982. *L'Excisée*. Paris: L'Harmattan.

Africa Women's Organisation, ed. 2005. *Training Kit. Prevention and Elimination of Female Genital Mutilation among Immigrants in Europe*. Vienna: AWO African Women's Organisation.

African Human Rights Law Journal. 2001. Vol. 1(2). http://www.chr.up.ac.za /centre_publications/ahrlj/journals/ahrlj_vol01_no02_2001.pdf (last accessed 1 June 2006).

Annas, Max and Annett Busch. 2005. "Ousmane Sembene's 'Moolade' [sic] Opposing Genital Mutilation." *Qantara.de Dialogue with the Islamic World*. Trans. from the German: Christina White. http://www.qantara.de/webcom/show_article.php/_c-310/_nr-179/i.html. April 22 (last accessed 1 June 2006).

Barnes, Virginia Lee and Janice Patricia Boddy. 1994. *Aman: The Story of a Somali Girl*. New York: Pantheon.

Beck-Karrer, Charlotte. 1996. *Löwinnen sind sie. Gespräche mit somalischen Frauen und Männern über Frauenbeschneidung*. Bern: eFeF Verlag.

Dariatou angesichts der Tradition. n.d. Brussels: GAMS Belgium.

Erben, Rita, dir. 2000. *Bolokoli—Mädchenbeschneidung in Mali*. SWR Teleglobus, Rita Erben Filmproduktion.

"Female Genital Mutilation and Obstetric Outcome: WHO Collaborative Prospective Study in Six African Countries." 2006. *The Lancet*. June 3. 367(9535):1853–41.

Gillette, Isabelle and Marie-Hélène Franjou. 1995. "Femmes assises sous le couteau: Manuel destiné à l'animation de réunions ayant pour thème la prévention des mutilations génitals féminines." Edition GAMS, Paris.

Hosken, Fran. 1993. *The Hosken Report. Genital and Sexual Mutilation of Females*. Fourth revised edition. Lexington: WIN News.

———. 2000. *The Childbirth Picture Book*. Lexington, MA: WIN News.

Kahn, Joseph P. 2006. "Fran P. Hosken, 86; Activist for Women's Issues Globally." *The Boston Globe*, February 12, Obituaries. http://www.boston.com/news/globe/obituaries/articles/2006/02/12/fran_p_hosken_86_activist_for_womens_issues_globally/ (last accessed 1 June 2006).

Khady. *Mutilée*. 2005. Mesnil-sur-l'Estrée: Oh Editions.

Levin, Tobe. 1986. "Women as Scapegoats of Culture and Cult: An Activist's View of Female Circumcision in Thiong'o's *The River Between*." *Ngambika. Studies of Women in African Literature*. Eds. Carole Boyce Davies and Anne Adams Graves. Trenton, NJ: Africa World P., 205–21.

———. 1999a. "Abolition Efforts in the African Diaspora: Two Conferences on Female Genital Mutilation in Europe." *Women's Studies Quarterly* 1 & 2. "Teaching About Violence Against Women." New York: The Feminist Press, 109–16.

———. 1999b. "Alice Walker: Matron of FORWARD." *Black Imagination and the Middle Passage*. Eds. Maria Diedrich, Henry Louis Gates, Jr., and Carl Pedersen. New York: Oxford University Press, 240–54.

———. 2003. "Female Genital Mutilation and Human Rights." *Comparative American Studies. An International Journal*. Special issue on human rights. Guest eds. Werner Sollors and Winfried Fluck. Vol. 1(3):285–316.

————. 2005. "Female Genital Mutilation: Campaigns in Germany." *Engendering Human Rights: Cultural and Socio-economic Realities in Africa.* Eds. Obioma Nnaemeka and Joy Ezeilo. New York: Palgrave Macmillan at St Martin's Press, 285–301.

Mackie, Gerry. 1996. "Ending Footbinding and Infibulation: A Convention Account." *American Sociological Review.* December. 61(6):999–1017.

Nour, Nawal. 2006. "The Healer." *The Boston Globe Magazine.* April 30, 18–9.

Nwapa, Flora. 1966. *Efuru.* London: Heinemann.

Rahman, Anika and Toubia, Nahid. 2000. *Female Genital Mutilation: A Guide to Laws and Policies Worldwide.* London: Zed.

Sahel Initiative Third Millenium, prod. 2000. *Stop Excision: For the Dignity of Women.* CD. Bamako, Mali.

Schuhler, Juliane, dir. 2005. *Ich war ein Nomadenkind.* In the series Lebenslinie. Bavarian Television, Germany. First aired 21 November.

Sen, Purna, Cathy Humphreys, and Liz Kelly with WOMANKIND Worldwide. 2003. "Violence Against Women in the UK: CEDAW Thematic Shadow Report 2003." *Womenkind Worldwide.* www.womankind.org.uk/upload/ CEDAW-report.pdf (last accessed 8 June 2006).

Walker, Alice and Pratibha Parmar, dir. 1993a. *Warrior Marks: Female Genital Mutilation and the Sexual Blinding of Women.* Video.

————. 1993b. *Warrior Marks: Female Genital Mutilation and the Sexual Blinding of Women.* New York: Harcourt, Brace.

Addresses

FORWARD-GERMANY e.V.
(Foundation for Women's Health, Research and
    Development)
Executive Director: Dr. Med. Vet Asili Barre-Dirie
asili.barre-dirie@forward-germany.org
Vice President: Fadumo Korn
fadumo.korn@forward-germany.org
Hohenstaufenstr. 8, 60327 Frankfurt am Main
Telephone: +49 69 1382 6078
0160/92589796

http://www.forward-germany.org
http://www.furatena.net/forward
http://www.forwarduk.org.uk/germany
http://www.faduma-korn.de

Reading Group Guide

Summary

As a child, young Fadumo roams the steppes of Somalia until, at the age of seven, she is brought to an excisor who cuts her genitalia to mark her rite of passage into womanhood. Following her circumcision, commonly called "female genital mutilation" (FGM) or "female genital cutting" (FGC), Fadumo suffers from severe complications and is painfully crippled. Ultimately her family sends Fadumo to Mogadishu to live with her uncle in order to receive the medical attention she needs.

In Mogadishu, Fadumo is introduced to a world of luxury far removed from the nomadic life to which she has been accustomed. She arrives at a time when her country is on the verge of civil war. Her uncle, the brother of the Somali president, lives a protected life of wealth and privilege and provides his niece with an education as well as access to medical care. Diagnosed with severe rheumatism brought on by the cutting, Fadumo visits doctors in her own country, Italy, and finally Germany before she finds one familiar with the complications of FGM.

After receiving treatment for her rheumatism, Fadumo stays in Germany and meets Walter Korn, who helps her to become comfortable with her body. She marries him and is ultimately able, after corrective surgery, to bear a child. She goes on to become an activist working against FGM.

Discussion Questions
1. Though primarily practiced in Africa, FGM is also practiced in the Middle East, among a few ethnic groups in India and South America, and by immigrants to Western countries. Considering that FGM is not a localized phenomenon, what did you know about it before reading this memoir? How did you learn about FGM? If you did not know about FGM, what made you interested in reading this memoir?

2. How did you respond to Korn's description of her cutting and how she felt about it afterward? Has this memoir affected your opinions regarding FGM?

3. FGM is regarded by its practitioners as an important initiation into womanhood for young girls; it is a powerful tradition that guides a woman's views about her body and her self. What initiation rite did you go through? How did it affect your view of yourself? What is your view of traditions in general? What other traditions do you uphold?

4. After her circumcision, Fadumo becomes severely ill. How does her illness affect her personality and her psyche? Why does it take so long for her family, both on the steppes and in Mogadishu, to realize how ill she is? At what point does she connect her illness with her circumcision? What immediate and gradual effects does this realization have?

5. Korn has a large extended family, some of whom take her in as she travels in search of medical help and some of whom have very powerful political ties. Discuss her relationship with key family members. How do these relationships affect her recovery? After

civil war breaks out in Somalia, how do these relationships affect her life and her German family? How does the civil war affect Korn's view of herself?

6. Fadumo's Uncle Abdulkadir tells her, "It's important that you should move easily in both worlds, the modern and the traditional." Discuss whether Korn is able to do this throughout her life. What, if any, are the specific moments when she favors one "world" over the other? In what moments does Korn have problems moving between the two worlds? What are her obstacles? How does she overcome these difficulties? Or does she?

7. Early in her memoir, Korn states, "Men travel, and women guard livestock and children. In Somalia, the relationship between the sexes is clearly defined." In what other ways does Korn define the relationship between the sexes? Is this relationship as clear cut in Somalia as Korn states, and is it only related to the jobs they do? How do you think Korn would define gender roles in Germany? How do you define them for yourself?

8. Korn states, "My experience had taught me that touching my body meant only torture." After marrying Walter Korn she decides to undergo surgery to reverse some of the effects of the FGM. How does her attitude toward her body change after the surgery? What role does Walter play in these changes? How does having a child change her view of her body?

9. How does Korn view her nationality? How does she view race? How do these views compare to those of her Somali family, Walter, and Walter's parents? Do Korn's views on nationalism and race change after her son is born? Do they change after the civil war in Somalia breaks out?

10. Korn's family is part of Somalia's political elite. What does Korn think about this connection as a child? How does it affect her

view of herself, her family, and her country? Do these views change when she is older and visits Somalia with Walter?

11. Korn talks about her activist work only very briefly at the end of her memoir. Why do you think she does this? Discuss Korn's entrance into a life of activism. When does Korn identify herself as an activist? How did becoming a German citizen affect her activism?